LIFE
SKILLS

HOW TO COOK, CLEAN,
MANAGE MONEY, FIX YOUR CAR,
PERFORM CPR, AND EVERYTHING
IN BETWEEN

Julia Laflin

RACEHORSE PUBLISHING

Racehorse Publishing books may be purchased in bulk at special discounts for sales promotion, corporate gifts, fund-raising, or educational purposes. Special editions can also be created to specifications. For details, contact the Special Sales Department, Skyhorse Publishing, 307 West 36th Street, 11th Floor, New York, NY 10018 or info@ skyhorsepublishing.com.

Racehorse Publishing™ is a pending trademark of Skyhorse Publishing, Inc.®, a Delaware corporation.

Visit our website at www.skyhorsepublishing.com.

10 9 8 7 6 5 4 3 2 1

Cover artwork by Shutterstock.com
Interior artwork credited in the back matter

Print ISBN: 978-1-63158-492-3
E-Book ISBN: 978-1-63158-494-7

Printed in China

Disclaimer
Neither the author nor the publisher can be held responsible for any loss or claim arising out of the use, or misuse, of the suggestions made herein.

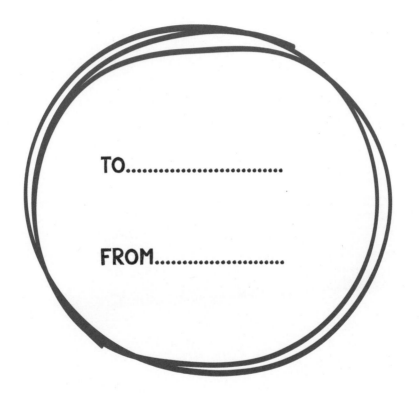

TO..............................

FROM..........................

CONTENTS

INTRODUCTION

Want to be that go-to person because you really know what's what? Then beef up your knowledge, add to your capabilities and include some new life skills in your repertoire.

Whether it's to save time and money, impress your friends, help someone out or to get yourself out of a jam, this book is made for you. There's a whole range of skills here to help you with both the down and dirty and the finer points in life.

Pick up a handy tip you might have missed, refine your sketchy understanding of a subject or try tackling some simple DIY. Learn how to handle yourself in a tricky social situation and how to secure a pay raise.

Keep this book on hand for when you need it, or check out the sections that appeal to you most. Whichever way you use it, start to build up your skill set now!

KITCHEN

Master these recipes and food storage
basics and you'll do nicely. There are also
nifty tips on choosing wine and opening
beer and champagne bottles, as well as
advice on how to deal with a kitchen fire.

BOIL AN EGG

You will need a small saucepan, an egg, a large spoon and a timer.

Fill the pan with sufficient water to cover the egg. Place the pan on the stove and bring the water to a rolling boil. Gently lower the egg into the water with the spoon and reduce the heat to a gentle boil. Cooking times are based on medium-sized eggs (for large eggs add 30 seconds extra):

- 6–7 minutes for soft-boiled.

- 9–10 minutes for a firmer set.

- 12–14 minutes for hard-boiled.

When done, lift the egg out of the water. For softer-boiled eggs, tap the top to crack the shell and prevent further cooking and serve. For hard-boiled eggs, drain the water from the pan and run the egg under cold water to cool it and prevent grey yolks.

HOW TO SEPARATE EGGS

Have two bowls, a saucer and a small cup ready. Carefully crack an egg onto the saucer. Place the cup over the yolk to contain it, then drain the egg white into one bowl. Tip the yolk into the remaining bowl. Repeat this process until all the eggs required are separated. Don't skip the cup and saucer process—one broken yolk in the whites will ruin the whole batch.

STORE FRESH FOOD

Follow the storage recommendations on packaged foods. The "best before" date is intended as a guide for when the produce will taste best. The "use-by" date on items such as fish, raw meat, cooked products and ready meals deserves close attention as it's these foods which could cause stomach upsets or full-blown food poisoning if the use-by date is not respected. Think of the "best before" as a quality guide and "use-by" as a health safety check. Make sure that you also finish these products within the stated time from opening—for instance, once opened use within three days.

- **Home-cooked foods and leftovers:** Cool down, cover and refrigerate.

- **Meat:** Store raw meat away from cooked foods and at the bottom of the fridge to prevent blood from dripping onto other food, which can cause food poisoning. Ensure that cooked meat is properly covered and refrigerated.

- **Fruit and vegetables:** Store in the fridge if not using straight away or you don't wish to ripen them. Onions, potatoes and apples can be stored on a surface away from direct sunlight or in a cool, dark place, such as a drawer or cupboard. Tomatoes should never be refrigerated as they will lose their flavor.

- **Eggs:** Once eggs are refrigerated they need to stay refrigerated, in order to reduce bacteria growth. The FDA requires all commercial eggs to be stored and transported below 45°F, so all eggs bought at commercial US supermarkets need to be stored in the refrigerator immediately.

- **Cooked rice:** Refrigerate as soon as it's cool—ideally within 1 hour. Eat within 24 hours, either cold from the fridge or reheated until the center is hot. Never reheat more than once.

Shops sometimes display goods in chiller units because they are best served cold and to give them the appeal of fresh food. If in doubt, keep it in the fridge at home.

FREEZE FOOD

Generally, food should be frozen on the day of purchase (although if it's stored in the fridge you can extend this time to nearer the use-by date). Most ready meals and packaged raw meat and fish come with instructions as to whether they are suitable for freezing. Follow the label recommendations for how long you should store food in the freezer. If you exceed this date, there will be a deterioration in quality and texture.

If you're buying food from a butcher or deli counter, ask the sales assistant if it is safe to freeze it. Sometimes raw products have been previously frozen, meaning there's an opportunity for unhealthy bacteria to grow if they are re-frozen.

It's OK to freeze meat and fish again once they have been cooked in a dish. As a rule, cooked leftover dishes, soups and stews freeze well. Ensure they're cold before freezing.

Use freezer bags with sealing clips or zip-lock tops and a permanent marker to label each bag. Clip tightly or fill to the top—don't leave an air gap. Use rigid food containers for soups and liquids.

Foods that don't freeze well:

- Raw foods with a high moisture content such as salad leaves, cucumber, watermelon or oranges, unless you plan to eat them frozen; they turn to mush when defrosted.

- Creamy foods like yogurt, cream and custard which will separate into curds and whey.

- Starchy foods like pasta and crumble toppings.

MAKE A SALAD DRESSING

You will need good quality olive oil, white wine vinegar or lemon juice, salt, Dijon mustard, runny honey and a clean, empty jam jar with a lid. This dressing will go well with any kind of leaf or raw vegetable salad; your friends will beg you for the recipe.

As a base, use three parts olive oil to one part white wine vinegar or lemon juice and put these into the jar. The oil coats the salad ingredients and the acid in the vinegar or lemon cuts through the oiliness and adds zing.

Add a pinch of salt, half a teaspoon of Dijon mustard and half a teaspoon of runny honey. If you don't have honey, dissolve half a teaspoon of sugar in a tiny amount of boiling water.

Put the lid on the jar and shake the ingredients to blend them. Taste and adjust, if necessary, by adding more of any of the above ingredients as required. This quantity will be sufficient for one serving bowl of salad.

You can vary the ingredients as you wish. Use red wine, balsamic or cider vinegar instead of white wine vinegar or lemon. Add a pinch of dried oregano or a grind of black pepper. Try grainy French mustard instead of Dijon.

Remember to give the dressing a good shake before you pour it over the salad as the ingredients will separate, or serve in a jug and give your guests a spoon for stirring. Any leftover dressing can be stored for up to three months in the fridge.

CHOP AN ONION

You'll need a chopping board and a sharp knife.

1 Place the onion on the board. Hold it steady and chop off both ends of the onion, about 0.5 inches in.

2 Peel off the brown, papery skin. If the first outer layer of white flesh is dry and tough, peel this off too.

3 Turn the onion onto one of its cut ends and cut it in half. Place each half face down on the board. It's the fumes from the exposed cut face of the onion that cause our eyes to water, so keeping the cut side facing the board will reduce onion tears.

4 Take half at a time and hold the edges of the onion firmly. Cut it into slices from right to left.

5 Then turn the onion 90 degrees on the board and cut in the same motion again from right to left, giving you neat, regular pieces of onion. The onion can become slippery, so cut any stray lengths individually for an even dice.

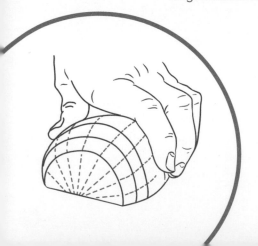

PREPARE AND COOK
A ROAST MEAL

Roast meals will need to be shopped for well in advance of your lunch or dinner plans to allow for cooking times, so plan your meat, vegetables and accompaniments ahead of time.

Roasting times and temperatures for meat will vary according to type and cut. Ask the butcher or check the package label if in doubt.

Plan your cooking times so all the food is ready at the same time. Start with the time the oven needs to go on for the meat, which is the element that will take the longest. Allow time to rest meat before carving. If your meat is cooking on a high heat, your potatoes will take about 1 hour to roast. Give them longer if you are slow-roasting the meat. Roast parsnips take about half the time of potatoes, whereas peppers and red onions take halfway between the two.

BEST ROASTED POTATOES

Peel and chop the potatoes into even-sized pieces. Place them in a saucepan of cold, salted water. Bring to the boil and cook until par-boiled—around 7–10 minutes, depending on size. Drain well into a colander and shake gently to rough up the outsides. Heat a generous tablespoon or two of goose or duck fat in a roasting pan in the oven until hot. Remove the pan from the oven, add the potatoes and use a spoon to coat each potato in the melted fat. Roast until crisp and golden, turning once during roasting time.

MAKE SOUP

Here's a simple, quick recipe to start with, which **only requires an onion, a can of tomatoes, chicken stock and thyme**.

TOMATO AND THYME SOUP

(Serves two. Prep and cooking time: 15-20 minutes)

1 Peel and finely chop an onion. Melt a pat of butter in a saucepan over a low heat. Then add the onion and cook for 5 minutes until soft and transparent.

2 Add a 14-ounce can of premium chopped tomatoes, a crumbled chicken stock cube, a splash of water and a pinch of dried thyme.

3 Cook for a further 10 minutes. Cool, before blending by hand or in a blender. Heat again to desired temperature. Season and garnish with a splash of olive oil, swirl of cream or croutons.

TOP TIPS

- Fresh stock or premium stock cubes give the best results. If you prefer to use vegetable rather than meat stock, add garlic for depth of flavor.

- Use seasonal vegetables for optimum flavor.

- Experiment with herbs and spices.

- Thicken soup with potatoes, bread, pasta or more vegetables rather than flour, which is trickier to control and can result in a lumpy texture.

COOK PASTA

You will need pasta, a large saucepan, water, salt and a colander.

1 Fill the saucepan with cold water, put the lid on and bring the water to the boil. Remove the lid and add a tablespoon of salt. Return the water to a rolling boil, add the pasta and stir once to separate it.

2 Spoon out one piece when it is 1-2 minutes away from the suggested cooking time. Cut it in half to see if it is cooked through. A white and grainy center means further cooking time is required.

3 Continue to test once a minute until the pasta is done. For *al dente* pasta—with a little bit of bite—remove from the heat before it is completely soft.

4 Have a colander ready in the sink, then drain the pasta into it. It is now ready to serve, or combine with sauce.

TOP TIPS

- Choose a large pot or saucepan as pasta needs plenty of room to move around while cooking.

- Allow 4 cups of water per 3.5-ounce serving of pasta. Salt generously.

- If combining pasta with sauce, heat the sauce before adding to the pasta unless it is an uncooked or oil-based sauce (such as garlic oil or pesto).

- Serve pasta into deep, warm bowls to keep it hot for as long as possible.

MAKE A BOLOGNESE SAUCE

Here is an adaptation of Italy's most popular pasta sauce. In this recipe ground lamb is suggested instead of the traditional ground beef.

(Serves six. Prep and cooking time: 40 minutes)

1 lb ground lamb

Splash of olive oil

1 large onion, finely chopped

1 large carrot, peeled and finely cubed

1 garlic clove, peeled and crushed

1 large glass of red wine

14 oz can chopped tomatoes

Pinch of *herbes de Provence*

Dash of Worcestershire sauce

1 tbsp of tomato purée

5-6 medium mushrooms, chopped

1 beef stock cube, dissolved in 1/2 cup of hot water

Heat the olive oil in a thick-bottomed saucepan over a medium heat. Add the onion and carrot and cook gently for 5 minutes, or until the onion is translucent and the carrot softened. Add the garlic and cook for a further minute.

Meanwhile, add the lamb to a hot frying pan and turn it quickly with two wooden spoons or spatulas. Brown until there is no visible raw meat. Drain the fat from the meat into a dish and set aside.

Add the browned lamb to the pan of softened vegetables. Add all the other ingredients and heat until bubbling. Turn down to a simmer and cook with the lid off for 30 minutes, stirring occasionally. If the sauce becomes too thick add a splash of water. Season with salt and pepper to taste.

Ladle onto cooked spaghetti and sprinkle with grated Parmesan.

STEAM VEGETABLES

Not only is steaming vegetables simple to do, but it comes with benefits: more nutrients are retained; soggy, waterlogged greens are a thing of the past; and there is no need for draining.

It's not necessary to invest in an electric or tiered stove-top steamer; a molded silicone basket or a folding metal one will do the job just as well, save you money and be less bulky to store.

First, place your steamer basket into a saucepan and fill the pan with cold water until it almost reaches up to the floor of the basket. Too much water and you will be boiling the bottom layer of veggies; too little and you risk boiling the water away, burning the vegetables and the pan. Prepare your chosen vegetable and place in the basket. Put the pan lid on, ensuring that it fits tightly to prevent the steam from escaping. Bring the water to the boil, then turn down the heat sufficiently to maintain the steam.

Most packaged vegetables from supermarkets state the number of minutes required for steaming in the cooking instructions. Alternatively, cook until stalks (or the densest part of the veggie) are soft enough for your liking; test softness with the top of a blunt knife. When the vegetables are cooked use a cloth to lift the steamer basket out. Tip the boiling water away, return the basket of veggies to the pan and replace the lid to keep hot until needed.

MAKE MASHED POTATOES

Floury, fluffy potato varieties make particularly excellent mashed potatoes. Although you can mash most potatoes, waxy types make it harder to achieve a good result and fingerling or new potatoes are often too dense for the job.

Discard any potatoes with green patches and dig out any sprouting eyes with the sharp end of a potato peeler. If you're not following a recipe, allow two to three medium-sized potatoes per person.

Skin on or off? It's your choice. If you're cooking a meal to impress then peel your spuds for an even texture and color. Or take the lazy option: leave the skins on and congratulate yourself on getting more nutrients.

METHOD

1   Chop the potatoes into equal-sized chunks and place them in a saucepan with sufficient cold, salted water to cover them. Put the lid on and bring them to the boil, then turn down the heat and simmer for about 15–20 minutes until the potatoes are soft through to their centers. Test this with a blunt knife.

2   Drain well, return them to the pan with a generous pat of butter and a splash of milk. Mash until smooth with a potato masher or fork, adding more butter and milk if necessary. Season generously with salt and pepper and serve.

3   If you are feeling adventurous, add herbs, garlic, cheese, grainy mustard or horseradish to your mash.

COOK A STEAK

Remove the steak from the fridge an hour before cooking so it comes up to room temperature. Rub the meat all over with olive oil and season with salt and pepper. Heat a thick-based frying pan or griddle. Make sure it is extremely hot before adding the steak (if you can hold your hand 6 inches from the pan/griddle for more than a second it's not hot enough). Once the steak has been added to the pan, turn the meat once a minute for even cooking until done as desired.

TOP TIPS

- The most popular cuts of steak are rump and rib-eye for depth of flavor, while pricier sirloin and fillet are chosen for tenderness.

- Fillet steak is cut thick so it may require a minute or so more cooking time. A steak served medium-rare to medium will be juicy and full of flavor. Cook for 6 minutes for medium-rare or 4 minutes for a thin steak. You can always cook steak a little longer if it's too pink but you can't undo it if it is overcooked.

- Well-done steak can risk being tough and dry; however, if you prefer not to see any pinkness to your meat then a longer cooking time will suit you. Allow 8 minutes in total, depending on thickness.

- Test the steak with your finger. A medium-rare steak will have a bit of give, while a well-done steak will feel firm to the touch. Once the steak is cooked, rest it on a plate for 2–4 minutes to allow the juices to flow. This settling process encourages a tender finish. Add a little extra oil or butter if preferred.

STUFF AND ROAST A CHICKEN

Hygiene is extremely important when handling raw chicken as it carries bacteria that are only killed off when the bird is thoroughly cooked. Throw away packaging carefully and wash any utensils or surfaces that have been in contact with the chicken with hot, soapy water—not forgetting your hands.

1 Heat the oven to 375°F.

2 Lift the neck flap of the chicken, at the end nearest the wings, and fill the stretchy skin with as much stuffing as will fit into it. Tuck the flap end under.

3 Place the chicken in a baking tray. Rub softened butter all over the breast and legs and season with salt, pepper and a sprinkling of herbs. Roasting time depends on weight. A 3-pound chicken will take around 1 hour and 20 minutes.

4 Check it's done by inserting a sharp knife where the inner thigh and breast meet. The juices should run clear with no trace of pink. Lift the chicken onto a serving dish or board and let it rest for 10-15 minutes before carving.

TRADITIONAL SAGE AND ONION STUFFING

1 Peel and finely chop a small onion.

2 Add in approximately 3.5 ounces of breadcrumbs, 1 teaspoon of sage (fresh or dried), salt and pepper.

3 Add enough water to bind the mixture together: around 2-3 tablespoons.

CARVE A ROAST

A sharpened carving knife is essential and a long carving fork is useful for steadying joints as you cut. A metal carving dish with prongs to grip the meat will also help to retain heat. Warm plates and serving platters in the oven for a minute or two to avoid dishing up lukewarm meat.

Rolled joints with no bones are the easiest to carve as they require simple vertical slicing along the length of the roll. Remove any string from slices before serving. For rolled pork, it's easier to remove the whole rack of crackling off the joint and break it into strips rather than attempting to cut straight through both at once.

Carve chicken by slicing vertically through one side of the breast, then cut vertically through the leg to create a drumstick and then at the thigh to give two leg joints. Detach the wing. Repeat on the other side. Slice any stuffing into sections.

Leg of lamb or pork is carved in small slices parallel to the big bone running through the joint.

For shoulder joints, use your finger to find the shoulder bone. Cut down into the meat on one side of the bone. Turn the knife to cut horizontally and remove the chunk of meat in one piece. Repeat on the other side of the bone before turning the joint over and cut the bone from the underneath. Trim off any remaining bits of meat. Carve the large pieces into slices against the grain.

HOW TO
GUT A FISH

1 Place the fish on its side on a chopping board (preferably one color-coded blue for fish), or on its back if it is a big fish. Wear latex gloves if you'd rather. Take a sharp knife and slice the fish open as shown.

2 Insert the knife through the gills and slit through the skin flap.

3 Holding the head in one hand, pull away the gills and the entrails, then scoop out any remaining guts, dark tissue lining and clingy membrane. Rinse out the cavity under the cold tap to remove any last small bits.

MAKE A STIR-FRY

Everyone loves a stir-fry. Simply throw all the ingredients into a wok and it's ready in minutes. You'll need a flat-bottomed wok if you're cooking with electricity, as the whole base needs contact with the heat source.

Basics for stir-frying from scratch:

- Preparing ingredients takes more time than the cooking.

- Prepare all the raw ingredients and line up everything else you need before you start.

- Arrange the ingredients in the order they need to be added: meat and hard vegetables need to go in before more leafy, watery veggies, as they need a longer cooking time; garlic, ginger and chili flakes can be added and cooked for a few seconds before adding any sauce.

- Chop hard vegetables like carrots into thin slices and cut broccoli stems lengthways.

- Noodles that need rehydrating can be cooked separately in boiling water according to the packet instructions and set aside until required.

- You'll need to keep stirring the ingredients for even cooking.

- Have bowls at the ready to enjoy your stir-fry as soon as it is cooked.

Once you get the hang of stir-frying, you can experiment with ingredients and there are many prepared components available to buy such as ready-cut vegetables, straight-to-wok noodles, seasoned meat strips and stir-fry sauces.

MAKE A PIE

If you're a pie-making novice, start with this easy recipe.

CHICKEN, HAM AND LEEK PIE

(Serves four. Prep and cooking time: approx 1 hour)

Shortcrust pastry
8 oz plain flour
3.5 oz cold butter, diced
Pinch of salt

Filling
1 tbsp of oil or butter
1 onion, chopped
2 leeks, trimmed
and sliced
1 large chicken breast and
1 large chicken leg joint,
skinned and cubed (or add
leftover cooked chicken
before the pie crust is
added)
2 large slices of ham,
snipped into strips
A dash of heavy cream
1 chicken stock cube
dissolved in 1 ¼ cup of
boiling water

Sift the flour into a large bowl. Add the butter and rub it into the flour with your fingertips until it resembles fine breadcrumbs.

Add the salt and 2–3 tablespoons of cold water. Ball into a firm dough. Wrap in cling film and refrigerate for 15–30 minutes.

Gently fry the onion and leeks in the oil or butter until translucent. Add the raw chicken cubes. Fry until the meat is white on the outside.

Add the ham and cream, then pour in the stock. Let this bubble and reduce a little.

Remove from the heat and transfer to a rimmed pie dish. Then heat the oven to 350°F.

Assembly and cooking

Sprinkle flour onto a clean, dry kitchen counter and onto the rolling pin to prevent sticking. Remove the ball of pastry from the cling film and start to roll it into a shape of even thickness, larger than the diameter of the pie dish. Lift and turn the pastry 90 degrees each time you roll to prevent it sticking to the counter. Add more flour if necessary.

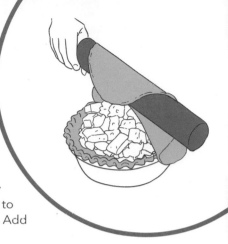

Brush the rim of the pie dish with a little water. Cut strips the same width as the rim of the dish from the edge of the pastry, leaving enough for the lid. Press the strips onto the rim of the pie dish until it is covered. Brush the strips with water. Lift the remaining pastry, which will form the lid, on the back of the rolling pin and onto the pie dish so it rests on the strips around the edge of the dish. Trim away any excess pastry.

With the tip of a knife press the lid on all the way round, then crimp and seal it.

Cut a couple of slits in the top of the lid to let the steam out. Brush with beaten egg or milk for a golden finish. Bake for 30 minutes.

ROLL A BURRITO OR FAJITA

1   Warm a soft tortilla wrap for 10 seconds in a microwave, or for about 10 seconds on each side in a hot frying pan.

2   Place the tortilla flat on a chopping board. Spoon your chosen filling onto it, placing it slightly off-center and nearer to you. Don't overfill as this will make it harder to roll and to eat without making a mess. Add any toppings or sauce.

3   Fold up the bottom over the filling, holding it in place with your fingers while you fold over the sides.

4   Roll up from the bottom tightly, slightly squeezing back to compact the filling as you roll.

5   Press down as you work towards the end to help it stay together. Tuck under the end flap of the tortilla. Cut in half if desired.

MAKE A VICTORIA SPONGE SANDWICH

This recipe is fool-proof provided you follow it carefully. It really matters that you measure the quantities accurately, use the prescribed size for the baking tins and DON'T open the oven door during the cooking time.

(Serves eight. Prep and cooking time: 40 minutes)

12 tbsp butter, softened

about 1 cup golden caster sugar (or regular white caster sugar, if golden is not available)

3 medium eggs

1.5 cups self-raising flour

Strawberry, raspberry or other fruit jam

Whipped cream

Powdered sugar to decorate

Heat the oven to 355°F

Cream the butter and caster sugar together in a large bowl with a hand mixer until they are pale in color. Then add the eggs, one at a time, to the creamed mixture. Beat well.

Sift the flour into the mixture and fold in lightly with a spatula.

Grease and line the bottom of two 7-inch round cake tins. Divide the mixture evenly between the two. Place both tins on the same oven shelf. Bake the sponges for 25 minutes until risen and golden brown. To test they're done, press the middle of each cake lightly to check the surface springs back a little.

Remove from the oven and let them stand for 1 minute before turning out onto a wire rack to cool. Once they are cold, sandwich the sponge cakes together with jam and whipped cream. Decorate the top with sifted icing sugar.

MAKE TEA

Good quality tea will make the best "cuppa." For the ultimate tea-drinking experience choose the most premium loose-leaf tea that you can afford, even if you save it for weekends or special occasions. Find a good independent deli or a tea shop where you can order a pot to "try before you buy" the type that most appeals to you.

Even if you use a teabag rather than leaves, it is worth brewing it in a teapot for better flavor. For loose tea it's handy to have a teapot with a fitted mesh insert; this allows room for the tea leaves to swell and lifts out for easy cleaning.

Fill your kettle with fresh tap water as you need. Don't be tempted to use old kettle water—the oxygen will have been boiled out of it and this will impair the tea's flavor. Just before the kettle boils pour a little water from it into the teapot and swill it around to warm it. Empty the pot and add your teabags (one for each person) or loose-leaf tea (one teaspoonful for each person plus one extra for the pot). Pour on the kettle water while it is still at boiling point. Pop the lid on the teapot and leave to brew for 2-3 minutes, or longer if you prefer strong tea. Pour into mugs or tea cups; thin bone china is a good choice for loose-leaf tea. Add milk and sugar as required.

MAKE COFFEE

A coffee capsule machine is convenient for making quick cups or Italian espresso but it is not the cheapest way of making coffee in quantity. Stove-top percolators, French presses or filter coffee machines all use ground coffee: buy this in packets then seal and store in the fridge once opened, or if you have a coffee bean grinder you can produce your own as required.

It's important to check the manufacturer's instructions for each device, but here are some general guidelines for each:

- **Stove-top percolator:** Load water into the bottom section and ground coffee into the middle container and assemble. Place on stove. As it heats, the water is drawn up the central shaft through the coffee to fill the top section with a ready-to-pour brew. It will make a bubbling noise when the coffee is ready.

- **French press:** Put one scoop of ground coffee per cup into the bottom of the French press. Bring a kettle of water to boil and allow to cool for a minute or two (boiling water scalds coffee and spoils the flavor). Pour in the correct ratio of water to coffee required. Stir. Fit the top on and leave to stand for 3-4 minutes before slowly pushing the plunger all the way down.

- **Filter coffee machine:** Fit a filter paper into the cone-shaped holder in the top. Scoop coffee into the filter paper and pour the corresponding quantity of tap water into the tank. Ensure the collecting jug is in position before turning the machine on. The coffee is ready when the machine stops burbling.

CHOOSE WINE

- Shop at a wine store where advice is readily available. Helpful, knowledgeable sales staff combined with shelf signs to give guidance are good starting points. Some shops will also let you taste certain wines for free; others encourage you to buy a selection of sample glasses of fine wines for a modest price.

- Supermarkets have some good selections and deals on mixed cases and half-cases, which are a good way to find favorites. Online wine companies and societies can offer a good choice for a regular commitment or modest joining fee.

- Look beyond sexy labels on the front of the bottle. Instead, focus on the words on the back to identify what you might like: dry, crisp, acidic, fruity, sweet, light, well-rounded, full-bodied, oaky and so forth.

- It's an idea to be wary of wines described as "table wine" as these are cheaper blends. They may be good but there is a risk that they will lack depth of flavor, or that they are unbalanced in composition.

- For complementary wine and food pairings, light wines tend to pair well with lighter foods like chicken and fish, while full-bodied wines go with richer foods such as red meat and strong cheeses. Contrasting flavors can match, too—check bottle labels for pairing guidance. Spicy foods work well with a crisp, acidic, white wine with a medium to low alcohol content.

WASH DISHES BY HAND

Use a dishwashing bowl if you're tackling more than a few items. This will save effort and water. Wear rubber gloves if you want to protect your hands.

Begin by scraping leftover scraps into the trash, then rinse the worst residue off plates, pots, pans and cutlery in the empty sink and stack to one side. Place the dishwashing bowl in the sink, add a squirt of good quality dish soap and fill with hot water. When the bowl is full but not overflowing, turn off the tap and begin to wash the dirty items with a brush, sponge or dish cloth.

Rinse items once they are clean with warm or lukewarm water (which should be directed into the sink, away from the bowl). Keeping warmth in the water helps the items to dry quicker. When you're done, wash the bowl inside and out with soapy water.

TOP TIPS

- Put dirty cutlery at the bottom of the bowl as you're running the water. It should be easier to clean once it has soaked a little.

- Start to wash china first with a brush, sponge or dish cloth, using the stream of hot tap water.

- To prevent breakages, wash glassware separately using cooler water.

- Change the water when it gets dirty and add more dish soap as necessary.

- Stubbornly stained oven dishes can be soaked and cleaned with scouring pads—but use a softer sponge if they're the non-stick variety. Use very hot water for this to cut through grease.

OPEN A BEER BOTTLE
WITHOUT A BOTTLE OPENER

This is a great skill to whip out when someone relocates the only bottle opener at a party.

Find something that can flip open the top, such as a spoon. The indented metal lock within a door frame will also work—try not to use the inside of a wooden door frame as it risks leaving an indentation. Most can openers have a bottle opener, so check this too.

If you're nowhere near the kitchen, try levering the top off with another beer bottle inverted against the teeth of the cap. A key, a thin coin, a flat-headed screwdriver, the edge of the arm of BBQ tongs, or a burger flipper will also do the trick—as will the square end of a lipstick case. Even a single sheet of paper will work if folded lengthways to a tiny flat strip, folded in half and the fold used as a lever.

Don't be tempted to use your teeth or a kitchen knife to do the job as this could result in an unwanted trip to the dentist or your local emergency room.

If you're a car owner, think about keeping a spare opener in the car for outdoor events and picnics. Or to save you the trouble next time, get a Swiss Army knife or a key ring with a bottle opener attached.

POP A CHAMPAGNE CORK

Provided the bottle has not fallen over or been shaken up, this technique should ensure that you can crack it open in style without spilling a drop (but have a cloth handy, just in case!).

With your champagne flutes at the ready, unpick a little of the foil around the bottle neck to access the flattened twist of wire which holds the metal cap in place (called the "cage"). Untwist the wire to loosen the cage but don't remove it from the bottle. Keep your hand over the cork to keep it safe, and be careful to not point it at anyone in the room or at anything valuable.

Grasp the bottle firmly by the base in one hand and hold the cork with the other. Make sure to keep the bottle at a 45-degree angle. Twist the base of the bottle gently keeping hold of the cork as it comes out—you will still experience the satisfying pop as it releases and see the appealing vapor wisps rise into the air. This is the most sophisticated way to open a champagne bottle and keeps you firmly in the driving seat.

Occasionally, the cork can be stubborn. If you come across resistance, alternate the twisting motion with a little upward leverage with your thumb, while keeping hold of the cork, until you achieve the desired result.

PUT OUT A KITCHEN FIRE

The kitchen is the most common place for a fire to start—with the most frequent cause being oil or fat left unattended, becoming too hot and igniting. Deep fat fryers can be a fire risk if not supervised closely when in use.

This type of fire can get dangerously out of hand in seconds so it's key to take the right action promptly to put it out. If it's already too big for you to deal with, get everybody out of your home, close the door behind you and call 911 for the fire department.

If the fire starts in a pan on the stove and is small, use an oven glove to move the pan off the source of heat and clamp the lid on—lack of oxygen will suffocate the flames. Turn off the stove. If the fire is bigger but still manageable, turn off the heat if you can reach the controls safely. A fire blanket can smother flames and put them out, as can a wet towel or tablecloth. Never pour water onto a fat pan fire—it can make it worse.

For a fire in a deep fat fryer or other electrical appliance, pull the plug out or switch off power at the fuse box. This may stop the fire immediately but if it doesn't, smother it with a fire blanket.

Deal with oven or microwave fires by closing the door and keeping it shut. Turn off the power and wait for it to cool down.

CLOTHES

In this section: become a whiz with your laundry, learn quick sewing repairs, vanquish stains and find great packing tips.

SEW

Keep a sewing kit handy for simple repairs. It should contain: needles, needle threader, white, black and a range of colored cotton thread, sewing scissors, pins and a tape measure.

Choose the color thread to match or contrast with the material you plan to sew by holding a single thread against the fabric. Cotton thread has a sheen to it, so you may need to go a shade darker. Use cotton thread on cottons, linens and other natural fabrics; match synthetic thread to man-made fabrics to prevent threads from breaking.

Select the right size needle for the thickness of fabric. Flatten the needle threader's diamond-shaped wire and feed it through the eye of the needle. Insert a length of thread into the diamond shape. Pull the wire back through the needle's eye and you're almost ready to sew. To avoid frustrating tangles, resist using too long a thread and keep the shorter end around 2 inches. Remember to adjust the thread as you go so that the short end isn't sewn into the fabric.

Next, you need a knot. Lick your forefinger. Take the end of the thread and wrap it round the tip of that finger so that it overlaps across your finger pad. With your thumb against your finger, roll the thread off and pull the roll down to form a strong knot at the base of the thread.

Once you're finished sewing, fasten off on the underside of the fabric by sewing four small stitches over the top of each other. Pass the needle through the loop of the last stitch before pulling tight and repeat this action. Cut the thread with scissors, leaving a tiny tail.

Backstitch creates a strong bond and is best for repairing seams.

Use **slip stitch** for hemming as it is almost invisible on both sides.

Overcast stitch contains fraying seams.

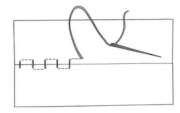

Basting stitch is designed to tack two pieces of fabric

together while you sew, in cases where pins won't hold them well.

SEW ON A BUTTON

Buttons have a habit of unravelling, so make sure to re-attach them before they come off completely and become lost.

1 Thread a needle with thread, either to match the button or other button threads.

2 Knot the end of the thread.

3 Pass the needle from the underside of the fabric through one of the tiny stitch holes from where the button was before.

4 Pull the thread all the way through so the knot is touching the back of the fabric.

5 Push the needle through any hole in the back of the button.

6 Move the button down the thread. Hold it in the correct position on the fabric.

7 Pass the needle through either the adjacent or opposite hole, depending on whether matching buttons have been stitched on diagonally or with parallel lines of stitching. Pull the needle out through to the underside.

8 Repeat the process so that threads pass through each of the button's holes four to five times.

9 Don't stitch the button on too tight or it will be hard to use. Wind the thread once around the underside of the button.

10 Fasten off on the underside of the fabric.

DARN A SWEATER

A stitch in time saves nine; catch a small hole in your favorite cashmere sweater or pair of woolen socks and the mend might be invisible.

With a tiny hole in a fine knit sweater, you may be able to get away with using cotton or embroidery thread. Knitted wool is forgiving and if you sew carefully, the darn will blend in with its surroundings. Otherwise, you'll need a darning needle and woolen thread that's the same ply and color as your garment and a darning mushroom (or equivalent).

Place a wooden darning mushroom beneath large holes to support the fabric. These can be purchased online or in sewing shops. Alternatively, you could use an orange or a lemon.

Thread your needle and stitch vertical support threads across the hole. Start the vertical supports well away from the hole to reinforce thin, worn wool close to the edges. Follow the lines of the knit, or the "v"s of stocking stitch, and incorporate any worn, ragged edges as you darn. Then weave in and out through those supports horizontally, always taking care not to pucker the stitches by pulling them tight. The horizontal rows of stitching can start nearer the hole. Use the needle to pick up alternate vertical strands to the previous row. When complete, remove the darning mushroom and fasten off on the reverse side.

HOW TO

PATCH A HOLE

To repair holes in the arms of coats, jackets and sweaters, buy leather or suede elbow patches that sew or iron on.

To patch a ripped hole in fabric, follow these steps.

1   Trim frayed edges from the hole with sewing scissors and cut it into a square or rectangle shape.

2   With scissors, at each corner clip a tiny slit 0.25 inches deep at an angle of 45 degrees.

3   Find a piece of fabric of matching weight to your garment to be the patch. Cut it to match the shape of the hole, leaving a 1-inch margin on all sides.

4   Before securing the patch to your garment, stitch the edges of the backing piece using overcast stitch to prevent them from fraying.

5   Place the patch behind the hole with the fabric right side up.

6   Pin the patch to the garment. Use a basting stitch to secure the patch round all four sides.

7   Turn the 0.25-inch edges of the garment neatly under so they create a frame round the patch, then press into place.

8   Backstitch the turned edges all the way round.

FOLD BEDSHEETS

Ideally, when you take flat sheets out of the washing machine you need another pair of hands to help you pull and fold them into shape, particularly if they are super-king size.

You'll need some room space. Find all four corners and ask your helper to take the top two corners, while you keep hold of the other two. Walk away from each other with arms outstretched until the damp sheet is taunt. Hold on tight to your corners while both of you give the sheet a couple of firm tugs, outwards and away from you both. This action helps to remove a lot of awkward creases and straightens the outer edges making ironing much easier. Walk towards each other, matching your corners. While one person holds all the corners the other can pick up the fold. Repeat the stretching and folding process one more time, then peg out on the line or fold to fit a drying rack.

Ironed bedsheets can be folded into the best square or rectangular shape to fit their storage space.

Fitted sheets are convenient to use, if a little tricky to fold. Place them on a large flat surface with the elasticated side pieces flapped over on top and smooth the material flat. Take one of the short edges to match up with the other one, tucking in any stray side-piece fabric. Repeat this folding action until the sheet is the desired size for storage.

DO YOUR LAUNDRY

Wash at high temperatures (140°F or above) to kill bacteria and keep whites brighter. Run the washing machine monthly on empty at 200°F to maintain performance.

Sort your dirty laundry into piles for separate washes:

- Whites for a hot temperature wash (bedding, towels, underclothes, tea towels, dishcloths, flannels).

- Colored cottons suitable for a hot wash (as above).

- Whites for a warm wash (shirts, T-shirts, skirts, shorts, jeans, trousers).

- Coloreds for a warm/cool wash (as above).

- Delicates for a cool/gentle wash (silk, lace, mesh, synthetic clothing).

- Woolens and silk (sweaters, scarves, gloves). Wash these by hand unless you have a hand-wash/woolens or silk setting on your washing machine.

TOP TIPS

- Colors will run on some clothes if they're not washed at the correct temperature.

- Wash similar colors together (i.e. light colors or dark colors).

- If clothes are only lightly soiled, select the quick wash function on your washing machine.

- Because of their absorbent nature, towels need less washing detergent than other items.

- Close zips and link up hooks and eyes so they can't catch on other items.
- Empty the machine as soon as possible after the load has finished to prevent clothes smelling damp.

DRYING CLOTHES WITHOUT A TUMBLE DRYER

If hanging clothes outside is not practical, a heated drying rack is a good investment. Pin pants, jeans and skirts at the waistband; shirts, tops and T-shirts should be hung from the shoulders or dried on hangers. Don't overlap clothing as items will take longer to dry. Dry woolens flat to keep their shape.

HAND-WASH CLOTHES

Some top-of-the-range washing machines include a gentle hand-wash program, but if you don't have one of these you'll need to know how to do it yourself.

You will need hand-wash laundry liquid, which is gentler on delicate garments and designed to require less rinsing than machine washing detergent.

Gather the garments that you want to hand-wash. Put the amount of detergent recommended on the bottle label into a clean washing-up bowl. For color-fast items, fill the bowl with water that is between warm and hot (comfortable enough to hold your hand in); use cool water for dark or brightly colored clothes that might leach color. Agitate the water with your hand to ensure the detergent is fully dissolved.

Immerse the items—not too many at a time—and use your hands to work the soapy water through them for a minute or so, paying attention to armpit areas and collars where odor and dirt more readily accumulate. Leave to soak for a few minutes if necessary.

Lift the clothes out onto the draining board and tip away the dirty water. Rinse out the suds from the bowl, fill with cool, clean water and rinse the clothes in this by moving them around. Rinse and repeat until the water is clear. Squeeze items gently to remove excess water and hang out to dry.

Roll woolens and other items that need to be dried flat in a large towel to absorb the remaining amount of water.

REMOVE STAINS

- Act fast to avoid permanent staining and use the right product for the type of stain. Wash after treatment.

- Soak blood stains in cold water immediately.

- Solvents are needed to treat substances that are not water soluble, such as paint, tar or make-up. Solvent products that specially treat stains are readily available. To treat a stain with solvents, place one pad of white kitchen towel, or a clean cloth, under the stain and use another one to dab at it with the solvent.

- Pen marks will lift off when dabbed with hair spray.

- Rust can be removed with white vinegar or lemon juice.

- Apply white vinegar diluted with water to grass stains.

- Soak acid food stains like tomato for 30 minutes in white vinegar. Rinse and put a little detergent directly onto the stain before washing.

- Talcum powder absorbs grease and oil marks on clothes or suede shoes. Pile on and leave for 20 minutes. Shake off the powder and bang out any residue by hand. Repeat for stubborn stains.

- If you're out and about, blot the worst off a food stain. Unless it's a dry-clean only item, dab with water to dilute—this makes it easier to wash out later. Don't rub at the stain as this will push it further into the fibers.

- Heavy-duty white cottons can be bleached to remove stains but delicate fabrics can't withstand this treatment.

- Stain removers can take out dye on colored fabric. Test on an inside seam before applying.

HOW TO
IRON A SHIRT

It's easier to iron a damp shirt but a good steam iron will make short work of a bone-dry one, too. The rest is down to technique. Remember to iron around buttons rather than over them as you work through these stages. Follow this order to avoid creasing areas already ironed.

1   Start by ironing the back of the collar. Flip the shirt over and iron the collar front.

2   Next iron both cuffs, inside first and then outside.

3   Iron the shoulders next and then the yoke between them. Fit the end of each shoulder in turn around the nose of the ironing board to make this easy (see image below).

4   Iron the back of the sleeves. Lay one sleeve at a time on the board, shape to straighten the seam and match any crease on top of the sleeve from previous ironing. Start ironing from the top of a sleeve, working your way down to the cuff. Turn the shirt over and iron the front of the sleeve in the same way.

5   Then iron the front and back of the shirt. Start with the right-hand front and feed the shirt over the board as you go, so you iron the back and finally the left-hand front. Wiggle around the front buttons with the tip of the iron (see image below).

6   If the back has a box pleat (a pleat which runs down the middle of the shirt), start ironing at the top of it while pulling on the bottom with your free hand to define the shape easily.

7   Finish by ironing the collar in half lengthways, as it would be when you wear it. Put the shirt on a hanger and button from the collar downwards.

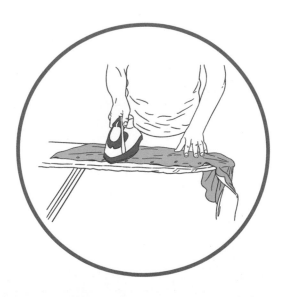

FOLD A T-SHIRT

1 Lay the T-shirt face down on a table. Smooth it flat.

2 Fold over one side and sleeve from top to bottom, taking a line between the collar and the shoulder seam.

3 Repeat the same action on the other side.

4 At this point, women's T-shirts can be folded in half. Men's T-shirts tend to be longer and benefit taking an extra fold before folding again into a square and turning over.

PACK A SUITCASE

- If you are traveling with carry-on luggage only you will need to pack liquids, gels and pastes in containers no bigger than 3.4 ounces—they'll also need to fit in one airport-issue clear, plastic bag that reseals easily.

- To avoid leaving behind something critical, create a list in advance to help you focus when you pack. An electronic list can be adapted to different types of vacations or business trips where core items remain the same.

- Air pressure can cause liquid toiletries to leak. Protect against this by wrapping items like nail polish, sunscreen and shampoo separately in small sealed plastic bags before zipping into a toilet bag.

- Fold clothes for special occasions around triple layers of tissue paper. This does a terrific job in preventing creases.

- Place heavier items such as shoes and toilet bags in the wheelie-end of suitcases to avoid crushing lighter items in transit.

- To save space, put clothes of the same size and shape together—for example, pile folded shirts or T-shirts neatly on top of each other. Alternatively, roll folded T-shirts together, stuff socks and underwear into shoes and fill in gaps with small items.

- Put shoes in shoe bags or plastic carriers if you don't want soiled soles to touch clothes.

- Consider packing valuables and key items such as electronic devices, chargers and important paperwork in your carry-on luggage in case your suitcase goes astray.

- Try not to over-pack; remember to leave room for a souvenir vacation purchase or two!

CLEANING

Take the drudge out of basic household cleaning when you employ these techniques. They include how to tackle domestic stains and the best way to spruce up your boots and shoes.

MOP A FLOOR

Before you start, select the right floor-cleaning product for the type of floor surface. For example, some wood floors may need to be cleaned with a particular product to protect their finish.

Stringy-headed or strip-cloth mops are good for floors that are tiled and ones with surface texture. These mops are best manipulated in a sweeping motion for optimum cleaning performance. Clean wood floors or linoleum with a sponge-headed or soft cloth mop, following the grain of the wood.

1   Clear the floor space: up-end chairs onto table tops; move small items of furniture like footstools and side tables out of the way and take up rugs.

2   Sweep or vacuum the whole floor to clean up dust, crumbs and hair.

3   Fill a bucket with warm water and the recommended amount of floor-cleaning fluid.

4   Dip the mop into the bucket to let it draw up the cleaning solution.

5   Lift the mop and allow excess water to drip back into the bucket before starting to mop. Or, if the mop is the squeezy-sponge type, use the handle mechanism to press out the surplus. This avoids wetting the floor more than necessary.

6   Start in the corner of the room furthest from the door and work in small sections, mopping towards yourself. Rinse the mop frequently, changing the water if necessary.

7   Keep people and pets off the floor until it has dried.

VACUUM A ROOM ·

Ideally, carpets, rugs and other floor areas need cleaning once a week to stop dirt from building up, help to prevent allergy flare-ups and control clothing moths. Always dust a room before you clean the floor, as particles will inevitably drop downwards in the process.

Use the right tools for the job: hand-held vacuums are fine for small areas but you'll need something bigger to tackle a whole room. There are many lightweight, high-powered vacuum cleaners on sale as well as bagless, cylinder-style models.

Vacuum the room systematically, moving small items of furniture out of the way beforehand.

Make sure that you shift beds and large items of furniture away from the wall periodically to suck up the dust underneath.

Make good use of the attachments to lift dust and dirt from upholstery, awkward spaces and the gap between the floor's surface and the baseboard.

Vacuum in all directions, letting the vacuum head linger long enough in one place to shift dirt effectively. Most vacuum cleaner heads have different height settings for cleaning different surfaces. Cleaning on the right setting can make a huge difference to the end result.

Change your vacuum bag or empty your cylinder before they fill up or the vacuum cleaner will lose much of its efficiency. For the same reason, never re-use vacuum bags.

HOW TO
MAKE A BED

Why bother when you're going to climb into it again tonight? It's entirely a matter of choice but here are the plusses: a tidy bed makes the whole room look tidy; it's nice to come home to; it's a pleasure to climb into after a long day; and it can make you feel organized and in control.

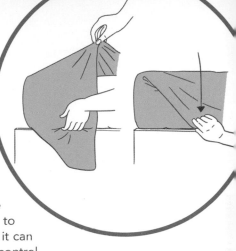

TOP TIPS

- Pull back the bedding while you're washing and dressing to let it air. Puff up pillows and shake duvets into shape before exiting the bedroom.

- Aim to change sheets, duvet covers and pillowcases once a week.

- Wash duvet covers inside out. Then when you make the bed you can put your arms through the opening, find and hold the cover's top corners, grasp the corners of the duvet cover's short sides and shake the cover over the duvet.

- If using unfitted sheets, place them so there is even fabric hanging down on all sides. Smooth and tuck the surplus fabric top and bottom before securing the sides with hospital corners—the best way of keeping the bottom sheet secure (see image). Puff up the pillows before putting the fresh pillowcases on them.

- If you prefer blankets to duvets, follow the same procedure for the top sheet and blankets as you did for the bottom sheet and fold the corners so they're secure.

CLEAN A WINDOW

Grimy windows are harder to clean, so to keep things easy clean all the glass twice a year and bring extra light into your home.

Clean windows on a dull day as strong sunlight can dry windows too quickly, leaving streaks.

Before starting, clear the space around the window you intend to clean. Protect the floor or surrounding furniture from water splashes. Remove dust and cobwebs with a brush.

Squirt a little dish soap into a bucket of warm water—too many soap suds are harder to wash off the window. Alternatively, add two tablespoons of vinegar to the water. Wet a sponge and squeeze well before you apply it to the glass to avoid drips. Rub the sponge over each pane, inside and out, to remove the dirt.

Purpose-made window cleaners can be sprayed directly onto glass and polished off, but strong versions can damage paintwork or soft furnishings.

Work a rubber-bladed squeegee down the glass from top to bottom in an S-shaped motion to push the water down and off the surface. Clean the blade from time to time with a rag to remove the dirt.

Use a clean, slightly damp microfiber cloth, chamois leather, or a worn-out T-shirt to take off any remaining water. An old trick of professional window cleaners is to use scrunched up newspaper to add sparkle and shine to dried windows, although you will end up with newsprint on your hands!

REMOVE CHEWING GUM FROM FURNITURE

There's a variety of ways to shift hardened chewing gum off furniture. Here are a couple that are simple to do and least likely to cause damage.

WOODEN FURNITURE

- **Oil method:** Soak a piece of paper towel or a clean cloth with vegetable oil and push it against all sides of the blob of gum. The oil should work its way under the edges and release the gum's grip. Polish off any residual oil once the gum has been removed.

- **Ice method:** Put some ice cubes into a small plastic food or freezer bag. Hold the bag against the gum to freeze it solid. Then lever the gum off the furniture with a blunt knife, being careful not to dig into the wood.

UPHOLSTERY FABRIC

- **Sticky tape method:** Strong duct tape is the best type to use for this job. Cut a piece and apply the sticky side to the gum to pull it away from the fabric. Keep repeating with clean pieces of tape until all the gum is gone.

- **Ice method:** Using ice to freeze the gum should also work on furnishing fabric. After the ice has worked its magic—and if the fabric is washable—finish with a little warm, soapy water then rinse and pat dry. If the gum's stuck to a cushion cover, take the cover off the pad before treating.

GET STAINS OUT OF A CARPET OR UPHOLSTERY

UPHOLSTERY

If fabric is removable and washable, sponge the stain with cold water or soak the fabric in a bowl of cold water for approximately 30 minutes. Treat with pre-wash stain remover before machine washing according to the fabric type.

For fixed furnishing fabric, blot the stain as much as possible. Mix a small squirt of dish soap with cool water so it's not too soapy and sponge the stain with a clean, white cloth. Blot up all the liquid and repeat the cleaning process until the stain has disappeared. Sponge with cold water to remove any soap and blot dry.

CARPETS

Act particularly fast on red wine stains! Blot the stain continuously with dry, white paper towel until you can't see any color on the paper. Remove a shoe and press lightly with your foot on the paper towel to help blot. Don't rub, as this will set the stain further into the carpet fibers. Add a little water and continue to blot. This technique can be employed for any type of liquid carpet stains.

For food stains, gently lift off thick spills and chunky pieces with a blunt knife before attempting to blot. Use diluted dish soap (as directed in the "Upholstery" section above) or spray with a good carpet stain remover, following the manufacturer's directions. Repeat if necessary. Vacuum when the area has dried.

CLEAN A TOILET

Don't just flush and run when you've been. Check the toilet to be sure it's in a pleasant condition for the next person. Take the long-handled toilet brush, usually found in its holder beside the toilet, and scrub away any stubborn residue or streaks left after flushing. Tap the arm of the brush against the side of the seat to shake off drips before transferring back to its holder. It's considered good manners to leave the toilet seat down—and the lid, too—particularly after a longer visit!

Toilets should be deep cleaned once a week to keep germs and viruses at bay, or more often if there's been a virulent stomach bug in your household. Wear rubber gloves, kept for this purpose, if preferred.

Carefully squirt strong, thick bleach under the inside rim and round the toilet bowl, or use a special-purpose toilet cleaner for the job.

Leave this on for around 10 minutes to neutralize bacteria while you work on the outside of the toilet (including the flush handle and the area around the seat hinges). Work from the top down to the floor with toilet cleaner and a disposable cloth. Then clean all the seat surfaces, including the lid and the rim under the seat.

With the toilet brush, scrub away at any stains or limescale marks under the rim and inside the toilet bowl. Tip waste water from the toilet brush holder down the toilet. Add a little bleach to the bottom of the holder. Then shut the toilet lid and flush away the bleach.

It's a good idea to wash the sink and bathroom door handles at the same time.

CLEAN AN OVEN

This isn't a job that most of us relish, but it needn't be hard if performed at regular intervals and the sparkling result can be satisfying.

First, check whether your oven has an auto-clean function (you may save yourself some work). However, even if it does, you'll still need to clean the oven racks. Remove these, including any vertical hanging racks, and soak them in hot, soapy water in the sink.

For manual cleaning, start by wiping away any loose debris. Then either spray on the chemical cleaner or try a more eco-friendly version (suitable only for lightly soiled ovens); leave it to work for the prescribed time with the door shut. Always check which cleaners are recommended for your oven make and avoid putting any cleaner on the element.

Alternatively, try the steam-cleaning method. You will need the bottom rack in place for this. Fill a large baking tray or oven-proof dish with water and place on the rack. Turn the oven on at its highest temperature setting. After 30 minutes turn the oven off and leave it to cool with the door shut. Then take a damp cloth and wipe down the inside, not forgetting the inside of the door. The steam will have done a good job of loosening grease and grime so this should be easy.

POLISH LEATHER FOOTWEAR

Not only does shiny footwear make a good impression but regularly cleaning your shoes and boots will extend their lifetime. Dirt and water from the street stains and dulls leather—and unless it is fed with shoe polish it also loses its waterproofing, dries and cracks.

Put together a shoe kit: tins of wax polish to match the color of your leather footwear; cleaning cloths or rags; two bristle shoe brushes (one stiff and one soft); and a cotton duster or microfiber cloth for polishing. Add a wire suede brush if you have suede items.

It's more efficient to clean multiple pairs of footwear at a time. Spread an old towel or newspaper over the surface on which you want to work, roll your sleeves up and consider wearing an apron with a bib while you work: shoe polish stains are difficult to remove.

First, ensure your shoes are clean. Wipe leather surfaces with a dampened cleaning cloth to remove all dirt, being careful not to over-wet the leather. Work around the stubborn outer edges and the heels with the cloth until they are clean.

Make sure the leather is dry before applying polish generously with a cloth or rag. Work it into the surface, particularly around any creases and seams. Leave on for 10 minutes. Then use the stiff brush to remove the excess polish, brushing vigorously until there is only a thin coating left. The brush will become stained, so only ever use this brush to take off the polish. Buff with the softer brush to encourage shine before finishing off with the duster or microfiber cloth.

POLISH FURNITURE

Beeswax polish protects unvarnished wood furniture and internal doors from splits and cracks, often caused by exposure to central heating. Proper application also helps build up protection against spills and stains and gives a pleasing mellow shine that can last for months.

Natural creamed beeswax polish is easier to apply than solid wax polish. Use a soft, clean cloth to apply it, rubbing with the grain of the wood as you work it over small areas at a time. Shine by rubbing with a separate clean cloth.

Resist buying spray polishes: these are silicone-based to give shine but they don't nourish the wood and can even cause it to dry out. Once silicone has been applied it is practically impossible to remove it without stripping off the whole surface of the wood and it can produce a milky look as it builds—rather like bloom on old chocolate.

HOUSEHOLD

If you're not a DIY aficionado by the end of this section, at least your "how-to-fix-it" knowledge will be ahead of the pack.

HANG A PICTURE

DIY SAFETY WARNING: Before taking any sort of tool to a wall, or making a hole in it, check what's behind the surface by scanning the area with a multi-purpose digital detector: this will indicate if there are any pipes, cables or studs where you're about to work. Either try to borrow one, as they are expensive to buy, or download an app to your phone.

A common mistake is to hang artwork too high. The center of the picture, or group of pictures, should be at eye level when you stand and look at it—but of course this depends how tall you are! Art galleries measure 57 inches from the floor as standard.

1 Consider where you want your picture, gauging its relationship to doors and furniture and the length of the wall space. Have someone else hold the picture in place while you stand back and check the position. Use a tape measure to be accurate in positioning its distance from other adjacent artwork and objects.

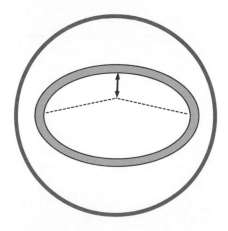

2 Also test that the picture hook will be concealed by the picture by suspending the hanging wire on the hook and letting it take the weight (see image on adjacent page). Mark your chosen position in pencil on the wall. Thread the nail through the eyelet of the hook and hammer it into the wall at a 45 degree angle.

3 A single hook is fine for small, lightweight pictures. For a bigger picture choose a double picture hook. For a heavy one, you will need a screw and a standard drywall anchor to secure the screw (see image below). You'll also need a power drill to make any impression on a masonry wall. Drill a hole big enough to take the anchor. Fit the anchor into the hole, making sure it is tightly embedded and flush with the wall. Choose the type of screw that has a head to hang the picture on and insert it.

PUT UP A SHELF
WITH BRACKETS

Note that if the wall is made of drywall, you'll need to locate the stud partitions and anchor your shelf brackets to them. Make sure you are confident there are no cables behind the wall; you can download a digital detector app to your phone to help you do this.

Match your shelf and brackets to support the weight of the load you intend them to hold. You'll need a stronger set for heavy books than for ornaments or cosmetics.

Hold the shelf against the wall and, with a pencil, mark where the bottom of the shelf should go. Use a level for perfection. Do the same with the brackets, spacing the distance between them equally.

Place each bracket straight against the wall, with the long side pointing downwards, and put a pencil mark in each fixing hole.

Drill holes in the wall where the brackets should go, using a wall plug on a masonry wall (see "How to hang a picture"). Insert screws into the bracket holes and secure the brackets to the wall.

To fix the shelf onto the brackets: place it on top, center it and pencil mark the underneath through the fixing holes. Remove the shelf and drill small, shallow holes where you marked. These are guide or "pilot" holes. Put the shelf back on the brackets and, to be sure they don't come right through to the top surface, use short screws to connect the two together.

HOW TO

REMOVE A NAIL AND FILL HOLES

REMOVE A NAIL

A claw-end hammer is the right tool for extracting nails from a wall or floor.

Slide the claw under the nail head so the nail is held in the "V". Use a sideways rocking motion to lift and work the nail out of the surface. The outer edge of the claw can dent and damage a wood floor or a decorated wall, so perform this task slowly and carefully; alternatively, slide a thin strip of wood or a ruler under the claw edge before you start.

FILL A CRACK OR HOLE

Ready-mixed fillers come in different grades to suit the holes you need to fill—from fine-surface fillers for small cracks to the deep-repair type.

Dampen a crack before you fill it to prevent the filler from drying too quickly and shrinking. Apply the filler with a palette knife, pressing it into the crack. Once dry, sand down excess filler with sandpaper wrapped round a block of wood.

To fill a nail hole, give it a light bang with a hammer to push any rough edges back into the hole. Apply general-purpose filler and sand when dry.

For large holes it's better to build up layers of filler, letting each one dry thoroughly before applying the next.

PREPARE A WALL FOR PAINTING

Painting a room is relatively quick to do and the finish can look professional if the preparation is done well.

Move all the furniture to the center of the room and cover with old sheets, disposable dust covers or newspaper to guard against paint splatters. Cover the floor well with similar protection, taping protective coverings to the floor edges before painting skirting boards to protect the floor from paint drips.

Dust walls and all paintwork—including chair rails, picture railings, moldings and baseboards—to prevent particles from clogging up the new paint. Wipe down kitchen and bathroom walls with a sponge and soapy water to remove grime and grease and leave to dry before painting. Fill cracks or holes with filler (see "Fill a crack or hole" above) and scrape away any cracked or flaky paint.

Protect window frames, baseboards, picture rails, light switches, wall light fittings and power outlets with closely fitting strips of masking tape. Take time to apply the tape carefully as this will allow you to paint the walls speedily.

PAINT A ROOM

Decide on your color once you've experimented with samples. Cover a large area of the walls with two coats of the sample color and wait for them to dry before you make your final decision. Remember, the color will look different on a wall in direct light.

Choose the type of paint finish to suit the room: satin and gloss paints are cleanable and therefore good for kitchens and bathrooms; eggshell is popular for walls in rooms with less wear and tear. Make sure you buy enough paint for the job—dark colors and patterned paper can take three coats to cover. Bare plaster will also need a coat of primer.

Stir paint before starting so the color is evenly mixed. If you're using a roller, cover your paint tray in foil or tight-wrapped cling film before adding paint to make the clean-up op a cinch. Tip enough paint to fill the well of a paint tray a third full. Load the roller with paint by dipping in the tray and rolling it on the flat part of the tray to remove excess paint. Don't over-saturate the roller or the paint will run and drip.

Always start with the ceiling. Use a paint brush on corners, edges and round light fittings first before using a hand-held paint roller for bigger areas. Use an extension pole on the roller to reach up high. When painting walls work systematically, with a "W" action, blending the paint evenly.

Remove all the masking tape when the paint is dry and leave the windows open to disperse the fumes. Clean brushes and roller equipment in cold water if the paint is water-based. For oil-based paint, soak items in turpentine.

CHANGE A LIGHT BULB

Switch off the lamp or light fitting and be sure the bulb is cool before removing it.

Unscrew the bulb from the socket—or if it has a bayonet fitting, hold the bulb and push it in and turn counter-clockwise until it releases. Do this with a firm grip on the bulb and a gentle action to avoid shattering the glass.

Replace with a new bulb, making sure it has the recommended wattage for the fitting to prevent overheating or scorching fabric shades. Screw firmly into place—or for the bayonet type, line up the twin prongs of the bulb over the two slots in the fitting, push them in and twist the bulb clockwise into place. Turn on the light switch to check that it is working.

Exceptionally long-lasting, eco-friendly bulbs (LEDs) are rapidly replacing compact fluorescent light bulbs (CFLs)—the early green solution to traditional incandescent light bulbs. These newer LEDs can last up to 35 times longer.

To change a downlight bulb, flick the light switch to the off position. Get a sturdy ladder, and some newspaper to protect carpet from a possible soot shower. Most fittings are spring-loaded and just need grasping round the outer rim with your fingers and pulling down gently, while supporting the light bulb. Ease the old bulb out of its socket and fit the new one in. Nestle it into the fitting and push it back into the ceiling.

For light fittings situated in tall ceilings or high landings you may need an electrician's help.

ASSEMBLE FLAT-PACK FURNITURE

Work in the room that the furniture is intended for and give yourself some space. You may need someone else to help hold things in place. Allow plenty of time, don't rush and follow this logical process.

1 Remove all the packaging with care and move it out of the way, unless you wish to use a sheet of the cardboard to protect your floor surface. Locate the instructions and check that all the parts, fixings and assembly tools listed are present. Set aside screws, bolts and other small parts in separate piles or containers.

2 Read through the instructions before you attempt to put anything together so you have an overview of the various steps.

3 Working methodically will minimize the opportunity for mistakes to creep in. Follow the steps, checking your work matches the instruction diagrams as you complete each section. When there's a choice of pieces or screws that are almost identical, except for the sizes, double-check you have the right one for the stage you are on—this is one of the most common reasons for flat-pack disaster.

GROUT TILES

This is the satisfying part of finishing off a tiling job. Once tiles are adhered to the wall or floor surface, the grout fills in the gaps in between the tiles and is necessary to stop them rubbing and cracking.

Ready-mixed grouting is a good buy as the consistency is pre-balanced. If you choose to mix up your own, aim for the same consistency as toothpaste. Work on a section at a time and use a grout spreader to work the grout mixture diagonally across the surface of the tiles. As you spread the grout across the surface of the tiles, it will be pushed into the gaps.

When the grout starts to set in the joins, run the flat edge of the spreader across the tiles again to remove the excess. Wet a sponge and squeeze out the excess water. Wipe it across the tiles to clean the area before starting a new section.

UNBLOCK A GUTTER

Rain pipes and gutters can block up with leaves, twigs and mud and the first you'll know about it will be when gushing, over-spilling water during a heavy downpour reveals the problem. Neglect to clean these essential drainage systems and you'll risk damp seeping in, damaging the walls or the roof.

Hoppers (protective coverings with holes that allow rainwater through while keeping debris out) or balled up chicken wire can be fixed over the top of rain pipes to stop blockages from happening.

If the blockage is in the rain pipe, a drainage rod, which is available from DIY outlets and hardware stores, can be fed into the rain pipe and manipulated to clear debris. A stiff piece of wire can work on an angled pipe.

For gutter cleaning, most first-floor gutters are accessible with a household ladder and can be cleaned out by hand using strong rubber gloves, followed by hosing with water if possible. Sometimes it's also possible to access a gutter from a window above. A telescopic golf ball retriever makes an inexpensive tool for scooping up rotten foliage and other detritus in these circumstances.

Call in a professional for any height over one story; many window cleaners also offer gutter clearance as a service.

UNBLOCK A DRAIN

Prevention is better than cure! Stop blockages before they happen by adhering to a few basic rules: never put fats or anything other than liquid waste down the kitchen sink and keep long hair from clogging the drains of showers, baths and sinks.

A plunger will remove blockages that occur within the first couple of feet of pipe below a drain. Place the plunger's mouth over the drain, grasp the handle and plunge up and down until the suction releases the debris causing the problem.

Rather than using a caustic cleaner for regular maintenance, pour a drinking cup of baking soda down the drain, followed by half a cup of vinegar. Leave this to fizz for 30 minutes before flushing it down with around two liters (about four pints) of hot water. Repeat as necessary.

For outside drain blockages that don't respond to the baking powder and vinegar remedy, you could try a few tablespoons of caustic soda (lye). Put this down the drain then add some water to make it fizz and see if the debris rises to the top. Remove the waste matter using rubber gloves.

If this doesn't work, you may need to borrow or buy a set of drain rods, which screw together clockwise. Wearing protective gloves, poke the rods into the chamber of the drain and slowly rotate them as you push them in. Remember to rotate them clockwise so they don't unscrew. After you've found the blockage and broken it up with the rods, flush the drain with water.

STOP AN OVERFLOWING TOILET

First, try shutting off the water supply: find the valve on the pipe below the cistern and turn the screw on it from the "12" position to "3". If the toilet is built in, it may be quicker to turn off the property's stopcock (often found under or by the kitchen sink, or in a front or back hall).

Keep a plunger handy in case your overflowing toilet is caused by a blockage in the U-bend. Make sure everyone in the household knows that diapers, pant liners and some wipes aren't flushable without consequences!

Sometimes it can be the ball valve inside the toilet cistern that is not functioning properly, so the water level may be too high in the tank. Remove the heavy porcelain lid of the tank (if the toilet is built in, remove the section of panelling covering the top of the cistern first). Flush the toilet and watch how the water fills in the tank. Modern tanks have a float connected to the tube that fills the tank; to adjust the flow, pinch the contacts on the side of the float and move them up and down (see image). For older-style mechanisms with a ball valve float that bobs in the water, try gently lifting the arm of the float to cure the problem or adjusting the screw on the lever of the float.

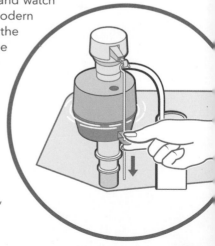

If none of the advice above works, consider calling in a plumber.

FIX A DRIPPING TAP

There are two types of taps: the traditional sort with two taps—one tap for hot water and one tap for cold—and the monobloc mixer tap. A constant drip from a traditional tap signals that a perished rubber washer inside needs replacing; if it's a dripping mixer tap, it could be the ceramic cartridge.

First, turn the water off; you can do this either at the stopcock or the valve on the supply pipes under the sink. Turn the taps on to drain off any water remaining in the pipes then plug the sink or bath hole so you don't lose any small parts!

For traditional taps, unscrew the top of the tap. Disassemble the layered parts, using a spanner to remove the nut that holds the spindle in place. Support the spout of the tap while you do this to prevent buckling. Untwist the spindle to access the bottom washer. If you don't already have replacement washers, take the spindle and old washers to a hardware shop to find the right kind. Fit all parts back into place with the new washers and restore the water supply.

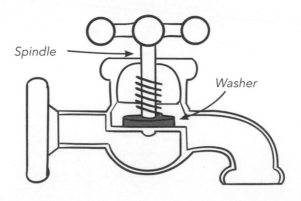

Spindle

Washer

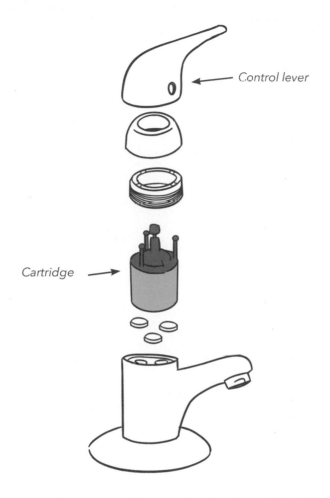

Control lever

Cartridge

The screw-on mixer tap cartridge tends to be tiny and located on the underside of the tap control lever. Follow the diagram to access the cartridge. If you don't already have a replacement cartridge, take the old one to a hardware shop so you can purchase the right kind. Put the tap back together as before with the new cartridge in place.

FIX A LEAKING PIPE

Turn off the water supply at the stopcock immediately, as well as the central heating boiler and the immersion heater. Then open every hot and cold tap to drain out any remaining water. If neighbors below or adjoining your property might be affected, let them know about the leak as this might give them time to lessen the chance of damage to their homes. Switch off your electricity at the mains if there is a possibility that leaking water might affect electrical wiring or fittings.

When the leak is caused by a loose joint, this can be tightened with a wrench.

Pipe with screw-on clamp

If the leak is in the pipe, there are a number of different pipe repair kits that can be purchased. These include, for example, specialist tape, self-tapping plugs that fit into the hole in the pipe and expand, or screw-on clamps. If in doubt about which to buy, take a picture of your pipe hole with your phone and show it to staff at your DIY shop. Follow the instructions supplied with your chosen kit.

You can also buy a new length of pipe. However, bear in mind that copper pipes must be soldered into place. If you're not confident with this type of repair, call a professional plumber.

Remember to refill your water system before relighting your boiler or turning on the immersion heater if you're fixing the pipe yourself.

BLEED A RADIATOR

Why, you may wonder, do you need to bleed a radiator? Properties fitted with gas fired central heating have water-filled radiators which sometimes accumulate air bubbles inside. This stops the water from being pumped around the system properly, leaving radiators lukewarm except at the bottom, and you feeling the chill.

To fix this you need to release the air with a radiator key. This is a short, sturdy key with big loops at the top forming an easy-to-turn handle and a square-shaped indentation at the other end. If you don't have one at home, they are inexpensive to buy from a DIY shop.

To avoid burning yourself, only bleed a radiator when the heating is turned off. Check the top of the radiator to see which end has a little square piece sticking out—this is the air valve to which you fit the key. Hold a cloth or some paper towel underneath the valve to catch any drips, then turn the key slowly counter-clockwise. You should hear a hissing sound as the air releases. When all the air has gone, water will start to drip or splutter out of the valve. At that point, turn the key clockwise to tighten the valve.

It's worth bleeding all the radiators to make your system work at its optimum efficiency. However, if this doesn't solve the problem, or you are having to do this more than once every few months, you may need to call in a plumber.

CHANGE A FUSE

Fuses are safety devices that prevent circuits from overheating or catching fire by breaking the electrical current.

Most fuse boxes in houses contain the re-settable sort that just need a switch to be turned back on when the circuit has been tripped. The other sort of fuses found in the home are in electrical appliances or in fused connection units—for example, in the wall next to an oven.

It's handy to know about fuses, because when an electrical appliance stops working it doesn't necessarily mean that it's died completely— it might just mean you need to replace the fuse. Standard fuse ratings are 3, 5 or 13 amps. Always replace a fuse with one of the same amp rating. They cost very little to buy in hardware shops, so keep a variety at home for emergencies.

Look for the fuse holder on the reverse side of the plug. Gently prise it open using a flat-headed screwdriver. Remove the fuse and replace it. In some older plugs, the back cover must be removed by unscrewing the large screw near the base of the plug to access the fuse. Screw the cover back on when the new fuse is in place.

Fused connection units contain ceramic fuses. Switch off the unit before using the screwdriver to remove the fuse holder, then change the fuse as described above.

PICK A LOCK

The vast majority of locks are tumbler locks. The notches on your key match up with spring-loaded pins of different lengths inside the lock's mechanism. When you insert the right key into a lock, the pins will be set to the correct height to allow the lock to rotate and release the door.

When you pick a lock, you're replicating the action of your key. You can buy a set of lock pick tools, or have a go with a couple of strong paper clips.

1   Unravel the end of one paper clip and bend to form a 90-degree angle.

2   Stretch out the other paper clip to form a straight line.

3   Insert the hooked end of the first paper clip into the bottom of the lock. Press downwards and pull it in the direction that the lock turns. It's imperative to keep this clip in place with the downward pressure on it during the whole procedure.

4   Push the straightened paper clip into the lock, all the way to the back.

5   Lift the straightened clip inside the lock and use a raking motion to scrape along the inside top of the lock as you pull it towards you. Success means you'll hear the pins clicking and the clip with the hook will turn easily to open the lock. Keep trying until it works.

NOTE: The advice on this page is only to be used if you have locked yourself out—not for breaking and entering!

USE BASIC HAND TOOLS SAFELY

- Keep sharp edges and blades covered when not in use. Be sure that shafts of hammers and axes are firmly connected. Wear protective clothing and footwear to guard against accidental contact.

- Choose the right size hammer for the job—too big risks a bent nail and injured fingers. Grip nails tightly and strike them squarely with the full hammer face, not the edge. Hold the handle near the end for greater accuracy.

- Keep a variety of flat and cross-head screwdrivers. Match their head size to the screw in question—it's safer for you and the screw head. Screwdriver handles can shatter when hammered; instead, use a chisel with the hammer and beware of flying chips.

- Use a wrench on bolt heads and the square shank of a heavy-duty screwdriver, never pliers. Don't push down on a wrench—it can slip and hurt you.

- Use a ripsaw at a 60-degree angle to cut with the grain of wood and a crosscut saw at 45 degrees for cross-grain jobs.

- Never use power tools around water unless they're made for wet conditions and don't carry them by the cord. Keep floors dry and slip-free while using electric tools. Tidy flexes so they don't cause trip hazards.

- Knock a small hole with a center punch and a hammer before using an electric drill. This lets the drill make proper contact with the surface, instead of wandering about.

RECYCLE AND MANAGE TRASH

Understand your local government's recycling policy, which can vary from district to district. Placing an incompatible or dirty item in the recycling can ruin a whole batch and incur substantial disposal costs for the council.

General rules for recycling:

- All items need to be completely clean and dry, so no empty pizza boxes or ketchup bottles with smeary necks.

- Most lids or bottle tops can't be recycled.

- Check labels on all plastic bottles, tubs and film for recycling symbols. Not all are suitable.

- Sometimes only certain components of packaging can be recycled—for example, tissue boxes where the cardboard is recyclable but not the plastic film insert.

Don't leave waste beside trash cans or let it overflow. Foxes and other local wildlife will rip into the bags and scatter the contents. Have enough strong galvanized trash bins with tight-fitting lids to accommodate all your food waste and other non-recyclables. Line them with bin liners to save on cleaning and to contain smells.

Rinse all household trash cans with disinfectant and water periodically.

For a fee, you can arrange a special collection by most councils for large items like old sofas, fridges or washing machines. Alternatively, post details on an online community recycling scheme in your vicinity where locals can come and collect your unwanted stuff for free.

DRY OUT A WET MOBILE PHONE/LAPTOP

The trick with all electronic devices is to let them dry out without pressing any buttons. Pressing them risks letting more water seep into the device, possibly causing irreparable damage, so employ restraint: it might save your gadget. It's equally important to remove the battery to prevent damage from short-circuiting, so on a device with a built-in battery you will have to press buttons to shut it down.

For phones, remove the cover, if there is one, and the SIM card. Dry the device with a towel or paper towel. Fill an airtight container with uncooked instant rice or couscous and bury your phone in the middle. Pop the lid on and leave the grains to draw out the moisture for 24–48 hours. It's important to be patient because if water remains now it may cause rust and corrosion later.

Laptops are more at risk from drink spillages, so it's sensible to keep drinks well out of range. A laptop might survive an encounter with a glass of water but the sugar content of fizzy drinks and wine could be your electronic lifeline's sticky end. Disconnect it from the power source and any cables. Once you've shut it down and removed any batteries, leave it open and turn it upside down; tilt to drain out the liquid. Keep it upside down while blow-drying it with a hairdryer on the "cool" setting for 15–20 minutes. Leave it in a good position to dry for 24 hours (maybe inside an airing cupboard) before attempting to turn it on.

LOOK AFTER CUT FLOWERS AND HOUSE PLANTS

When you buy or receive cut flowers as a gift it's important to put them in water as soon as possible. Submerge stems in a bucket or bowl full of water until you have time to prepare them properly for display.

Before arranging flowers, strip off any leaves that would otherwise sit below the water level—this helps keep the water fresher and slime-free. Cut the bottom off each stem on the diagonal with a sharp knife or some clippers, to give maximum opportunity for water to be absorbed up the stem. Add flower food if it's included with your bouquet to give your flowers a longer life. Position your arrangement in a cool place to make it last longer.

Drop a penny into a vase of tulips to keep them upright, or poke a small hole with a pin through each stem about 0.5 inches below the flower head.

Check the flowers at least every other day, if not daily. Some flowers are thirstier and may need a daily water top-up. Remove any wilted petals, flowers or leaves. Change the water and add more flower food.

Water and feed house plants according to the instructions that come with them and be sure to position them to fit their preference for light and shade. Avoid placing them in drafty spots in the winter months and protect furniture from water stains and leakage by standing plants on saucers, trays or impervious planter bases. Transfer them to bigger pots when they outgrow small containers.

VEHICLES

Here are your ready reference tips for trouble-free motoring and cycling, along with details of what to do if you hit trouble.

CHECK AND TOP UP THE OIL IN YOUR CAR

It's worth checking the oil level of your vehicle every couple of months if your car is an old model. The consequential damage to the engine if it drops too low can be severe and horribly expensive.

You will need a pair of rubber or latex gloves and some paper towel. Your car needs to be parked levelly and the engine cold before you start—this means waiting 30 minutes if you've recently driven it and 10 minutes if you've just re-parked it. Have the right engine oil for your car and a funnel handy, in case you do need a top-up.

Open the car hood (check your car's manual if you can't find how to do this) and disengage the safety latch to open it fully. Pull out the support strut and hook it into the roof of the hood.

The oil dipstick should have a brightly colored handle. Pull the dipstick out of the tube it's lodged in. Wipe the oil off with a piece of paper towel. Insert the dipstick fully back into the tube. Take it out again. If the oil level is correct, the oil on the dipstick should be between the MIN and MAX markings.

Top up the oil if necessary, using the funnel. Pour slowly and be careful not to overfill as this can be damaging to the engine. Avoid spilling any oil as it is harmful to the environment if it gets into the ground or waterways.

HAND WASH A CAR

- Never leave bird droppings or insect remains on your car's bodywork as these are corrosive. Soak or wash them off with water and a cloth, but don't rub too hard.

- Household detergents can be too harsh for cars. Only use the cleaning agents recommended by your vehicle's manufacturer. Different car parts can only tolerate certain cleaners. For the same reason, keep separate cloths for the different solutions used. Have clean drying mitts in your collection and avoid dry, coarse or rough cloths.

- Clean the wheels first, one at a time. Use a brush on the tire treads. Rinse as you go.

- Next clean the roof and upper body panels, then work your way down to the dirtier bottom panels. Use two buckets of water—one to wash and one to rinse as you go. Change the water frequently. Rinse with a garden hose if you have one.

- Use specialist car glass cleaner on interior and exterior glass rather than domestic glass cleaner. Wash plastic headlight lenses with windshield washer fluid that's safe for plastic.

- Dry and wax for ultimate shine and protection.

- High pressure cleaning jets need to be at least 1 foot from the car and not aimed directly at tires, electrics, seals, joints and trims.

- Shake out interior mats, vacuum carpets and upholstery, wipe the dashboard, trims and steering wheel with a safe cleaning agent. Artificial leather can be rubbed gently with a damp cloth dipped in a 1:100 dilution of dish soap and water, then left to dry. Wipe genuine leather covers with a damp cloth.

HOW TO
CHANGE A CAR TIRE

Check that you have a properly inflated spare tire, a jack and the vehicle's tool kit. These are usually stored under the floor of the boot and in adjacent compartments.

If you are on a gradient, check that the handbrake is on and wedge the unaffected tires from the front or behind as appropriate.

Remove the wheel's hubcap according to your car manual's directions. Loosen the wheel nuts with the wheel wrench but don't remove them completely. (If you have locking wheel nuts, use the key provided in the locking wheel kit to slacken the nuts.)

Next, fit the jack as directed in the car's manual. It's important to do this correctly so that you don't buckle the bodywork. Wind the handle until the wheel is raised a couple inches off the ground. Remove the loosened wheel nuts, then pull the tire off the car.

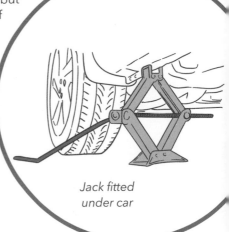

Jack fitted under car

Put on the new tire, tighten the wheel nuts and lower the jack. Check that the wheel nuts are fully tightened and the hubcap replaced before driving away. Remember: the spare tire is designed for emergencies and short-term use afterwards. Stow the damaged tire and tools in the trunk until you can take it in for repair or buy a new one.

CHANGE WINDSHIELD WIPERS

Change your wipers at least once a year. It is easier to replace the complete blades, rather than just the rubber inserts. Most cars have the U hook type of blades but check your vehicle's manual for instructions before you attempt to remove them.

Take the old blades into the shop with you when you go to buy the new ones and check whether they're compatible with your car's make and model before you purchase. You may be surprised to find the driver's side wiper is longer than that of the passenger's side; this is normal.

Change the blades with the wipers stopped in a vertical position on the windshield. Half-turn your ignition on to position the blades.

Carefully lift a blade away from the windshield until it clicks into a right-angled position, then turn the blade until it is at a right-angle to the wiper arm. Depress the small clip that joins the blade to the wiper arm while moving the blade downwards and then upwards to unhook it. Gently lower the arm against the windshield. Repeat with the other blade.

To fit the new blades, hold each one at right-angles to its wiper arm, feed it through the gap in the arm and push it upwards into the U hook until it clips into place.

Replace the wiper blades outside the shop you bought them from in case you need assistance. Don't throw away your old wipers until you are sure the new ones work.

JUMP START A CAR

Find yourself someone with a vehicle and a set of jump leads to help you out.

1 Park the assisting vehicle so the jump leads will reach between the two vehicles. The two vehicles **must not** touch.

2 Switch off your ignition and all electrical devices of both cars. Connect one end of the red positive lead to the positive terminal of your battery. Connect the other end of this lead to the positive terminal of the donor battery.

3 Connect the black negative lead to the donor battery first, then attach the other end to an unpainted metal surface of your car, away from the battery (e.g. a metal strut for the bonnet). Check all four grips are secure.

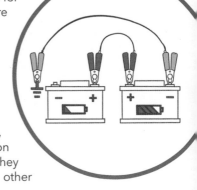

4 Start the engine of the donor vehicle and run it at idling speed. Let it run for a couple of minutes then start your car's engine.

5 Remove the negative jump lead, then the positive one, disconnecting from the battery on your own vehicle first. Make sure they don't touch each other or any other metal surface.

6 Drive, or leave your engine running for 30 minutes. Have your battery checked out at your garage workshop.

Note: Don't attempt a jump start if either vehicle has an electronic starting system or is fueled by anything other than gas or diesel.

CHECK YOUR CAR'S TIRE PRESSURE

Keeping tires properly inflated is key to braking performance, grip and reduced fuel consumption. Check them once a month when you fill up with fuel.

How much air to add depends on your specific car make and model and the load you are carrying. A car heavily-laden with vacation luggage and four passengers will need more pressure than normal. Follow the manufacturer's recommendation in your car's manual.

Park next to the tire pressure gauge at a gas station. You may have to pay a small charge for this service. Find the tire valve sticking out of the wheel rim. Unscrew the cap.

Pressure is measured in pounds per square inch (PSI) and bar. The machine should display in both and may have a control button so you can switch to your preferred type of measurement. The plus and minus signs on the machine allow you to set the pressure you want.

Go around the car, attaching the tire pressure gauge's hose to each tire in turn. The machine will check the pressure that you set and pump in more air, as needed. It will beep and stop when the pre-set level has been reached. When all tires have been checked return the hose to the machine and replace the valve caps.

PARALLEL PARK

When you learned to drive, your instructor would have taught you how to parallel park. However, if you haven't had to do it much, here's a refresher.

1   Choose a space that is two car lengths long to reverse into— when you've honed your parking technique you'll be confident about tackling smaller spaces.

2   Drive up alongside the parked car in front of the space you're pulling into. Stop when the back of your vehicle roughly lines up with that of the parked car. Check your mirrors to make sure that it's safe to move, then indicate.

3   Put your car into reverse gear and move back, turning the steering wheel to the right if you're parking on the right-hand side of the road and to the left if you're parking on the left-hand side. This will point the rear end of your vehicle towards the curb at an angle. Don't turn too sharply into the curb because you'll only have to pull out and start again (plus you risk scraping the parked car).

4   Keep maneuvering back slowly. Aim the back corner of the car at the curb two-thirds of your car's length back into the space, before you turn the wheel the other way.

5   Now you are in the space, you can move the car forward or back to make sure that you don't hog a big space or box in either of the parked cars to the front of or behind you.

HOW TO
DRIVE IN SNOW

When snow is forecast and driving's a necessity, go prepared for the worst. Pack sturdy, non-slip boots, warm outerwear, a blanket, food and drink. Throw a shovel in the trunk and some old bits of matting or carpet for grip in front of the tires should you become stuck fast—gravel, sand or cat litter will also do the trick. A fully charged phone is a good precaution, as is a full tank of fuel.

TOP TIPS

- Stay on main roads. Conditions should be better.

- Drive with enough speed to maintain momentum but not so fast that you might lose control.

- Aim to drive smoothly—no sudden acceleration, braking or sharp turns.

- Steer your way out of trouble. Braking on icy roads can send the car into a dangerous skid.

- Reduce your speed before you go down a hill.

- Don't follow the car in front too closely. This allows extra space needed for slowing and stopping and will also avoid driving in the spray it throws up.

- Think twice about passing. Tire tracks create pronounced grooves in the snow so you'll need to steer out of these, over the snow heaped in the middle and back into them again; you'll need to be sure your vehicle can handle this.

- If your vehicle slides on ice, don't brake. Instead, turn your wheels in the direction that the rear of the car is sliding to regain control. However, be careful not to over-correct.

- If snow is falling and it is daylight, drive with dimmed headlights.

FIX COMMON BIKE PROBLEMS

RECURRING FLAT TIRES

Check the PSI recommended on the side of your tire to see if your tire pressure is too low. Otherwise, check for debris that might be present inside the tire, or whether the tube has been caught between the rim and the tire.

GRINDING CHAIN

A lack of lubricant will make the chain grate, which can be recognized by a grinding sound. Check the lubrication of your chain every few weeks. Alternatively, your chain may be worn or your derailleurs may need adjustment. Likewise, excess lubrication can cause the chain to skip and attracts dirt to the chain and cassette (the rear gears). Clean them both with a degreaser (available from bike stores) and a small brush, rinse and dry. Add one drop of lubricant to each roller while turning the cranks backwards two or three times. Wipe off any excess on the outer side of the chain as you continue to spin it.

WHEEL OUT OF ALIGNMENT

Readjusting a wheel that's been knocked out of alignment (out of "true") takes practice, so if you are not confident it's best to take your bike into trusted shop to fix this problem.

CHAIN KEEPS COMING OFF

The chain can come adrift if you pedal hard while changing gear. However, should this still happen when you pedal softly, seek professional help from a bike shop. They will need to adjust the front derailleur, which moves the chain from one chainring to the next—a small alteration can damage the works if you're not skilled at this.

FIX A BIKE PUNCTURE

You'll need a puncture repair kit and a bicycle pump.

Turn the bike upside down so it's only resting on the seat and the handlebars; remove any obvious cause of the puncture, like a nail, from the tire.

Take the wheel off your bike, disconnecting the brake first if applicable, and let out any air remaining in the inner tube by pushing up on the tire valve.

Use tire levers to ease the tire and punctured inner tube off the wheel: insert one lever between the tire and the rim and push down to lift the tire up. Run around the rim with a second lever to free the tire completely. Carefully lift the tube out of the tire.

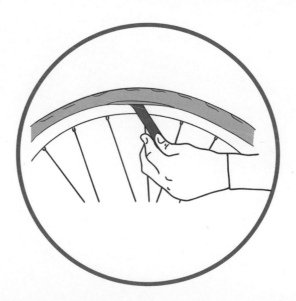

Run your fingers slowly along the inside of the tire, feeling for any remaining debris that might still be lodged in the rubber.Pump air into the tube until you can locate the leak, either by feeling or hearing the hiss of escaping air. Mark the hole with a pen and push the air out of the tube.

Sand around the area for repair with the sandpaper that comes in your repair kit. Spread a thin layer of glue over and around the hole and allow it to dry until the glue is no longer shiny.

Take a repair patch, peel off the backing and press it firmly into place over the glue.

Guide the tube back into the tire, aligning the valve with its hole in the rim. Push the tire back onto the rim with your hands, rather than tools, to prevent another puncture.

Reconnect the brake if necessary when you put the wheel back on your bike. If the rear wheel was removed, edge the chain round the gear cluster. The tire rim should be centerd between the brakes. Finally, re-inflate the tire.

THE GREAT OUTDOORS

Before you go adventuring make sure
you're well-equipped with these tips.

MAKE A FIRE

The key to a proper fire is laying it correctly.

1   Choose the spot for your fire, safely away from trees and bushes. Build a fire pit by digging a shallow depression, then surround it with rocks or large stones. The pit is optional but prevents flaming logs from rolling off the fire.

2   Gather your tinder (which should be fast-burning and easy to ignite, like paper or dry grass), kindling (quick to ignite, longer-lasting material such as large twigs, cardboard or small broad pieces of wood) and logs (more substantial pieces of wood to keep the fire burning, about the width of your arm).

3   Place your tinder in the fire pit then pile kindling over the top of it to create a loose pyramid shape. Leave a gap to light the fire with a match or lighter.

4   Light the tinder. Once the fire has caught well, add larger sticks and logs. You may need to blow lightly on the tinder to help the flames to catch.

TOP TIPS

- It's wise to keep a container of water nearby in case the fire gets out of hand.

- When you break camp, ensure that the embers of the fire are completely out. Scatter the ashes over a wide area and return the ground to its original state.

- The most common mistakes are adding too much stuff to the fire too soon, thus starving the flow of oxygen that it needs to keep burning, or trying to burn damp and unseasoned wood too early.

MAKE YOUR OWN GAS STOVE

Open fires are not allowed in some camping areas, which means cooking must happen over a portable camping stove. But you don't have to buy a camping stove if you know how to make your own out of a couple of empty tin cans. There's no need to buy a gas canister either as you'll be burning materials to produce gas naturally. You will, however, need to have a few DIY tools.

Find two food cans, one smaller than the other. Remove the lids of both cans with a can opener. Tip out the contents and save for later. Clean and dry the cans. Remove the labels.

Invert the big can on a table top and center the smaller can on top of it. With a permanent marker, draw a ring around the diameter of the small can. Punch a hole in the bottom of the larger can with a pair of sheet metal shears. Snip away the base from the punched hole to the marked circle. Smooth the edges with a file.

Towards the other end of the large can, drill a series of holes with a small drill bit around its bottom perimeter. Drill a second lot of holes above and in between the first row. Then enlarge all the holes with a bigger drill bit.

Using the small drill bit again, pepper the whole bottom of the small can with evenly spaced holes. Now drill a ring of small holes on the outside of the can, round the perimeter closest to the bottom. Repeat the same procedure as with the large can—drilling a second, alternate row and then enlarging them. Then drill a ring of smaller holes round the top edge of the small can.

Fit the small can completely inside the big can, bottom to bottom, and you're good to go! Fill it up with twigs, pine cones and other natural materials. Light with a match and start cooking straight away.

Use outside only and directly on soil, concrete or a heatproof surface as your stove will become extremely hot.

HOW TO
MAKE A BASIC SHELTER

Carry a ground sheet with you to create a basic shelter. They're windproof, waterproof and light to transport. The reinforced holes round their borders are designed for pegging and easy tying.

METHOD ONE

You'll need a rope for this. String the rope between two trees growing close together. Throw the ground sheet over the spine made by the rope and secure to the ground on either side.

METHOD TWO

As well as a ground sheet, you'll also need a small saw, a knife and a length of cord.

Cut three sturdy, straight branches into long poles: two of them need to be the same length (about 6 feet) and roughly the same diameter; the third can be about a foot and a half shorter. Cut one end of each pole at an angle to make them easier to drive into the ground.

With the cord to hand, plant the angled ends of the two longer poles firmly into the ground so that they cross over at the top when they lean towards each other. Wedge the shorter pole into the ground, to make a triangular shape with the base of the other two poles, and secure it to the crossover with the cord. It helps if this pole has a fork at the top to support the crossover from underneath.

Attach the center of the ground sheet's long side to the crossover. Spread it over the forked branch. Peg the sides and bottom of the sheet to the ground with sticks.

METHOD THREE

Follow method two above, but cut a longer third pole to form a spine. Cut pairs of decreasingly shorter branches to cross and tie into the spine. Cover with the ground sheet, or use branches with dense foliage.

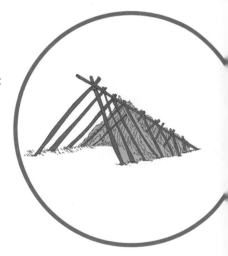

PURIFY WATER

There are many ways to make water safe to drink. Here are some of them.

BOILING

This is a reliable method but may not always be the most convenient. Bring the water to the boil over a campfire or stove, in a pan or heatproof container, and keep it at a rolling boil for 10 minutes.

WATER FILTERS

Drip filters have a pouch, rather like a medical IV drip, and use gravity to drip the water through a filter. The water can then be sucked through a plastic hose. Survival straws are a robust form of drinking straw attached to a lightweight water filter to let you drink as you go. **Pump-action filters** push water from one tank, through a filter cartridge, into the clean water tank on demand. These can come with large capacity tanks for group camping.

DISINFECTING TABLETS

Tablets are either iodine- or chlorine-based. Depending on the type, they can take from around 35 minutes to 4 hours to purify water. Iodine tablets work faster but they are not recommended for pregnant women or people with thyroid problems. All tablets tend to leave a disinfectant after-taste, particularly the iodine ones, but it's possible to remove this effect with neutralizing tablets.

GO TO THE BATHROOM IN THE WILDERNESS

Leave no trace when you have to go in the big outdoors.

Choose a private spot well away from water, your campsite or footpaths. Dig a hole 6 to 8 inches deep. Do the deed and use toilet paper—it's biodegradable. Re-cover the hole with any leaves or ground cover that was there beforehand. Don't worry if you see worms or insects in the top soil—leave them there, as they will break down your waste. Cleanse your hands with sanitizer gel.

When the ground is frozen or you're on rocky terrain you'll need to pack a poo kit consisting of newspaper, a plastic bag and a leak-proof container. First, lay the newspaper on the ground and go to the toilet on this. When you've finished, bag it up and place it in the leak-proof container. Don't forget to dispose of it when you return to civilization.

NAVIGATE WITH A MAP AND COMPASS

Place the compass on the map. With one of the straight outer edges of the compass, line up point A (where you are) with point B (where you want to go), being sure that the "direction of travel" arrow is pointing towards B.

Keeping the compass firmly in this position, turn the compass housing ring so that "north" and the red hatched orienteering arrow both point to the top of the map—making sure that there is no metal around you that will interfere with your compass arrow's magnetism. (Don't worry about what the floating compass needle is doing when you do this.)

When you are convinced that the compass housing is correctly aligned to the north, remove the compass from the map. Holding

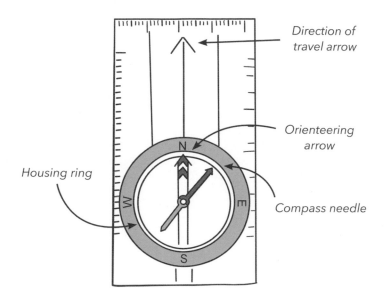

Direction of travel arrow

Orienteering arrow

Housing ring

Compass needle

N

W

E

S

the compass flat in your hand, turn yourself around until the red compass needle aligns itself parallel to the lines inside the compass housing area. Be sure the needle is pointing to north, not south, to avoid setting off in the opposite direction.

Walk in the direction of travel, holding the compass with the red compass needle matching the red hatched orienteering needle as closely as possible. To get your bearings, fix your sight on an immovable, distant feature in the landscape that's in line with your direction and walk towards it. Once there, check you are still on course, pick another landmark and walk towards that. Repeat this until you reach your destination: point B!

ESTIMATE HOW FAR
YOU HAVE TRAVELED

It's handy to have a measure of the distance you've traveled in case you're off target. Understanding how far you walk in a day, or a given number of hours, can prevent you from missing meal stops or overambitious expeditions that sap pleasure and morale.

Measure your pace before you set off. Calculate the distance it takes you to do a double stride and pace this out over 100 yards. Double stride counting as you walk is less counting to do on the journey! Repeat until you feel you have a good average to work with, remembering that slopes and uneven ground can shorten your normal pace.

On the other hand, you can time how long it takes you to walk between two spots. Again walking conditions can affect your speed, and inclines and descents will have an impact on timing out in the field.

HOW TO
CHOP FIREWOOD

Wear jeans with boots or shoes for this job, not shorts and sandals. For big logs, invest in a decent splitting maul (a long-handled, heavier version of a traditional axe) weighing no less than 8 pounds. This will chop logs along the wood grain without requiring too much strenuous effort on your part.

Use a broad-based log as a chopping block. Place the first log to split on top of it. For rapid results hook a length of chain round the circumference of your log, connected to a bungee cord. This can be adjusted to fit different sizes of log. This holds the log in shape while you work and keeps the pieces together when you move them to your wood stack.

Touch the blade of your maul to the top of the log, around halfway between the edge and the center and where there is a crack in the grain. With your feet planted squarely on the ground, fix your eyes on the area where you want your first strike to be. Raise the maul straight above your head with both hands. Pull it downwards with bent knees, using your legs to add power. Move yourself round the log, chopping at regular intervals so the log resembles a sliced-up pie from above.

Note: You will need permission from landowners to collect wood for fuel, or a licence from the U.S. Forest Service for national forests.

CARVE A PUMPKIN

Choose a pumpkin with a flattish bottom that doesn't list too much to one side.

Mark out your chosen design on the side of your pumpkin. The skin and flesh can feel a bit tough to carve through if you've never done it before. Select a simple pattern, like a grinning face, until you've gained some experience.

Draw a neat circle round the outside of the pumpkin's stalk to indicate where to cut out the lid. Make the lid big enough to allow you to scoop out the flesh from inside and to be able to drop a tealight or LED light into the floor of its base.

Use a serrated knife to remove the lid. Scoop out the pulp and seeds with a large spoon or an ice cream scoop.

Hold the pumpkin steady with your free hand while you carve out your design with the serrated knife. Use a sawing motion to cut out the shapes as cleanly and safely as possible.

Once you've finished the decorative part place your tealight inside, ensuring there's enough oxygen to keep it burning. If in doubt, cut a few extra holes in the pumpkin. Flickering LEDs can be effective and don't burn out.

TELL A GOOD GHOST STORY

Do it in the dark. Create the right atmosphere before you start and your audience will be ready to immerse themselves in your tale— seated round a campfire with their backs to the dark unknown behind them makes a good setting. Candlelight or low lamplight works in indoor shelters, particularly if the wind is howling outside.

Seek eye contact with the individual you are spinning your story to, keeping your voice low and speaking slowly—these techniques will help to keep them engaged as you build up to the finale.

Tell or adapt a story to fit a location that your listeners know, or one that you all walked past that day—the graveyard of the church, the house with the bricked-up windows, the old mine shaft, the copse on the hillside, the dark pool deep in the woods… Make one up if you're feeling brave but ground it in reality rather than fantasy and you'll be more likely to wind your audience into a state of suspense.

Weave your story round darker, more primal elements like water, winter, decay, death or animals.

Aim to subtly frighten rather than terrify. A suggestion of terror rather than full-on scariness is much more effective. Evoke unease by describing a whisper, a rustle, a shape, a shadow, a smell or a sensation and let your listeners' imaginations do the work for you.

PADDLE A CANOE ON YOUR OWN

Station yourself in the seat closest to the middle, facing towards the stern. Hold the paddle with one hand on the top and the other gripping just above the blade. The top of the paddle should remain at eye level. Here are the basic strokes you need to know.

FORWARD

On the side of the canoe nearest your lower hand, reach the paddle blade forward and into the water until your arm is fully extended. Pull the submerged paddle blade through the water until it is behind you. Rotate your shoulder forward and back with the direction of the stroke (rather than your spine). Pull the blade out of the water and repeat. Keep the paddle as vertical as possible by ensuring that your top hand is out over the water.

BACK

This is the reverse of the forward stroke. Put your blade in the water behind you and pull it through the water to the front of you.

COURSE CORRECTION AND TURNING

Paddling on one side continuously will turn the canoe round in a circle. For a quicker, more controlled turn, use a series of "J" strokes. This a useful stroke for correcting your course every few strokes, instead of having to change the paddle over from side to side. At the end of a forward stroke, as your arms come backwards, rotate your top hand inward towards the boat and down, and your lower arm slightly outwards to make a "J" in the water.

PRY

To move the canoe sideways away from an object, angle the paddle under the side of the canoe nearest to the object you want to move away from. Your top hand should be furthest away from you. Then pull the handle towards the boat until the paddle is vertical in the water.

DRAW

To move the canoe sideways towards an object, reach the paddle out and away from where you are sitting and into the water. Pull the paddle through the water towards you until it is vertical.

FIRST AID

The advice provided in this section is intended for guidance only and is no substitute for proper first-aid training.

If you would like to take a first-aid course, the Red Cross offers a wide range of training courses across the country. For further information go to www.redcross.org.

PREPARE A FIRST-AID KIT

Always have first-aid basics at home, plus an extra stock of band-aids and wound wash/antiseptic cream to hand in the kitchen. Check it regularly; discard any medicines that are past their use-by date and restock those items.

Find a suitable box, zipped bag or plastic container to hold all the items. Store it in a cool, dry place safely away from children. Tell everyone in your household where to find it.

What to put in your basic first-aid kit:

- Sticking band-aids in assorted sizes and shapes.
- Crepe bandages.
- Gauze pads in assorted sizes.
- Triangular bandage to create a sling.
- Sterile eye dressing.
- Adhesive tape.
- Safety pins.
- Scissors.
- Tweezers.
- Antiseptic wound wash spray and antiseptic cream.
- Pain relievers.
- Thermometer.
- Antihistamine cream and tablets.
- Skin rash cream.
- Eye wash and eye bath.
- Hand sanitizer.
- First-aid instruction book.

A first-aid kit kept in the car, or taken on vacation, can be useful for when you're away from home. You might want to add these items:

- Instant ice packs.
- Distilled water for washing larger wounds.

HOW TO

HELP SOMEONE WHO'S CHOKING

Encourage the person to cough up the obstruction in the first instance.

The next step is to slap them on the back between the shoulder blades five times with the heel of your palm, while you help them to lean forward.

If the victim can't speak, cry, cough or breathe, it's serious. Without first-aid assistance they will become unconscious.

The next remedy to try is known as the Heimlich maneuver. Stand

behind the person and slightly to one side. Put your arms around them so your hands meet in the area between the bottom of their ribcage and their belly button. Form your lower hand into a fist. Pull sharply upwards and inwards up to five times.

Should this not clear the blockage, call 911 for help.

While you are waiting for help to arrive continue to alternate the series of five back blows with the abdominal thrusts. If the patient become unresponsive, start cardiopulmonary resuscitation (CPR) with chest compressions—see page 117 for details of how to do this.

IMPORTANT:

- Don't give abdominal thrusts to babies under one year old or to pregnant women.

- If you're alone and choking severely, dial 911 immediately and perform abdominal thrusts on yourself to try to dislodge the item.

HELP SOMEONE WHO'S HAVING AN EPILEPTIC FIT

A seizure happens when there is electrical activity in the brain; there are many different kinds. This is what to do if someone is having a convulsive (tonic-clonic or clonic) seizure:

- Don't move them unless they are in a dangerous place, but do move furniture and other objects away from them.

- Note the start and finish time of the seizure.

- If they haven't collapsed but appear confused or unaware, comfort them and make sure that they are not able to hurt themselves.

- Talk to them calmly and quietly.

- Support their head with something soft if they are on the ground.

- Loosen any restrictive clothing round their neck to help their breathing.

- Don't put anything in their mouth, including your fingers.

- When convulsions have ceased, turn them so they are lying on their side and stay with them until they've recovered.

The CDC advises you should dial 911 if it's the first time someone has had a seizure; the seizure lasts for more than five minutes; or if the person doesn't regain full consciousness, or has a series of seizures without regaining consciousness.

HOW TO
PERFORM CPR

If you're not trained in how to do CPR, or how to use a defibrillator, call 911 first as the trained operator can talk you through the techniques until the paramedics arrive. This is particularly important for children and infants as their CPR procedures are different to adults'. If you're not completely confident in giving rescue breathing then provide hands-only CPR.

To provide hands-only CPR you will need to perform uninterrupted chest compressions until qualified medical help arrives.

1   Make sure the person is on their back on a firm surface.

2   Kneel next to the person's upper body. Place the heel of one hand on the center of the person's chest and, with the other hand on top of it, press down by about 2 inches.

3   Keep your elbows straight and your shoulders above your hands.

4   Press down at a steady rate of 100–120 beats per minute until help arrives.

It's worth checking out a list of well-known songs with a tempo of 100–120 beats per minute and committing one to memory should you ever need to perform CPR. The Bee Gees' "Stayin' Alive" is a popular one, "Rumour Has It" by Adele and Justin Bieber's "Sorry" also qualify. Spotify has an extensive CPR playlist for subscribers, or search for "CPR songs" in your browser to find the one that you will remember the best.

PUT SOMEONE IN THE RECOVERY POSITION

This procedure is designed to keep an unconscious person safe until medical help arrives, provided the person is breathing and has no other life-threatening injury.

If they are lying on their back, kneel next to them. Take the arm nearest to you and place it at a right-angle to their body so their palm faces upwards (image 1). Lift their other arm, bend it at the elbow and position it under their cheek so their cheek is resting on the back of their hand. Hold it in place (image 2).

With your free hand, lift their knee that is furthest away from you and bend it until their foot can rest flat on the floor (image 3). From this position, you can roll them onto their side to face you (image 4). Start the roll by pulling carefully on their bent knee.

Once this is done, check that they can breathe properly and any blood or vomit from their mouth can clear. Tilt their head back and their chin forward to assist.

If you suspect a spinal injury, instead of tilting their head support it with both hands—one on either side—and use your fingertips to gently open their jaw, without moving their neck. Should you need to put them in the recovery position because you can't keep the airway to their lungs open, do your utmost to keep their spine as straight as possible. Other people can assist with this. Two people on each side of the person can help you keep them in a straight line from head to feet as you roll their body over.

Once the person is in the recovery position, dial 911 for an ambulance and check their breathing.

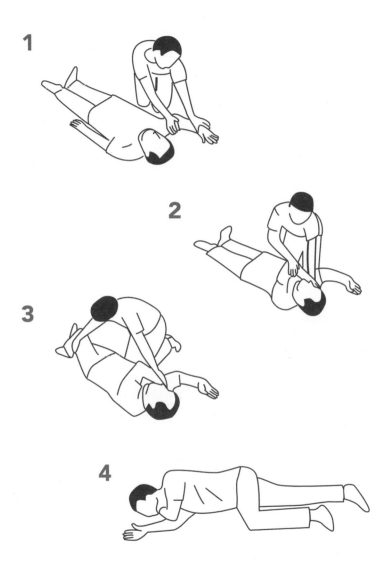

1

2

3

4

TREAT A MILD BURN

Mild, first-degree burn symptoms are redness of the skin, mild pain, swelling and skin peeling that occurs a day or so later. First-degree burns tend to heal after a few days; some may take longer depending on the part of the body that is affected.

Sunburn and scalds are the most usual causes of first-degree burns. Burns caused by exposure to electricity can have the appearance of a first-degree burn, but mask more damage below the surface of the skin, so always seek medical treatment for electrical or chemical burns and treat a burn as soon as possible to limit the amount of damage to your skin.

1   Apply cool or lukewarm running water directly to the burn for at least 10 minutes. Don't pour iced water or apply ice to the area as this can damage the skin tissue further. Creams or greasy ointments should also not be applied, although a thin layer of petroleum jelly or aloe vera is fine.

2   Take paracetamol or ibuprofen if the pain is bothersome.

3   Protect the burn from rubbing by taping a sterile gauze dressing lightly over it. Change this once a day as you wait for the burn to heal. Don't be tempted to break blisters that occur. An open blister can get infected.

4   Seek professional help for large or deep burns, burns of any size with white or charred skin and for burn blisters on the face, hands, arms, feet, legs or genitals.

TREAT A CUT OR WOUND

If the wound is bleeding, apply pressure with a sterile bandage or clean cloth until the bleeding stops.

For minor wounds, rinse the area with tap water. Clean around it with soap and water and a cloth but keep the soap out of the wound. Any particles of dirt and debris remaining should be picked out with sterilized tweezers. If you can't remove all the pieces, go to your doctor for treatment to stem the risk of infection.

Cover the wound with a plaster; for bigger injuries, use a sterile gauze bandage taped in place. To avoid infection, change this at least once a day or whenever the plaster or dressing becomes wet or dirty.

For more serious wounds, elevate the affected area above your heart while you stop the bleeding. Keep the compression on the wound even if blood is seeping through the bandage or cloth. Add more bandage or cloth on top rather than removing the first layer, as this can disturb the clotting process. For bleeding that continues for more than 5-10 minutes, call your doctor for advice. Go to your local urgent care center if your wound is more than 2 inches long, has a jagged edge, is a bite or has been contaminated with other matter.

Call 911 for an ambulance if you can't stop the bleeding or if arterial blood is spurting from the wound. Keep the pressure on the area until help arrives.

TREAT A BLISTER

The most common places for blisters to occur is on the feet and hands. Wearing new shoes or taking part in activities such as running or dancing can cause friction and pressure on the feet; gripping sports equipment like tennis rackets and golf clubs can blister palms and fingers.

The fluid that fills a blister is the body's way of protecting the tissue underneath from further damage. A burst blister, which can easily happen from further pressure to fragile skin, is painful and prone to infection if not treated.

As a precautionary measure, carry sticking band-aids or blister band-aids with you to protect, cushion and keep blisters clean. When you need to use a regular band-aid, don't apply it too tightly. Keep a bit of space in the middle to allow some air around the blister. Apply to clean, dry skin and change daily. Leave blister band-aids on until they fall off.

If possible, it's advisable to let your blisters heal without popping them.

CHECK FOR ABNORMAL MOLES

Pick a room with good lighting and remove all your clothes. Start at your head and work your way down your body. Check all areas of skin thoroughly, including your scalp, behind your ears, around your nose, between your fingers and toes and—not forgetting the great divide—your bottom! Ask a trusted friend to help you check areas that you can't see, or use a mirror.

The "ABCDE" of moles, used by dermatologists and other health bodies, classifies types to look out for:

- **Asymmetrical:** Normal moles are round and grow evenly. Melanomas expand at an uneven rate and are therefore asymmetrical.

- **Borders:** Unhealthy moles are prone to have ragged or blurred borders. Standard moles are rounder with clearly defined borders.

- **Color change:** A normal mole is the same color throughout. A melanoma can vary in color. If a mole becomes darker in color this is a sign that it is possibly cancerous.

- **Diameter:** Problem moles are usually larger than 0.25 inches but this is not a definite sign. Sizes of cancerous and normal moles can vary. Look for any changes in size.

- **Elevation or enlargement:** Moles that become raised, inflamed or swollen need to be professionally checked, as well as those that start to bleed, crust or itch.

Check any suspicious mole with your doctor, who can refer you to a dermatologist if they think specialist treatment is required.

CHECK YOUR HEALTH

Self-monitoring is a good way to keep an eye out for any changes in your health that might require medical help, as well as being a way of generally keeping you in fine fettle. Even if you are super-healthy be sure to register with a local doctor's office.

- Book regular eye tests at the opticians. Every two years is recommended.

- Ideally, visit your dentist twice a year for a check-up of your teeth and gums and for a clean by the hygienist. Dentists also check the health of the inside of your mouth—this is extra important if you smoke.

- A blood pressure reading of more than 90 over 60 (90/60) and less than 120 over 80 (120/80) is ideal. A higher reading might indicate a change in lifestyle is required. If your blood pressure tends to be higher than normal and requires regular monitoring, invest in a home monitoring device.

- Women aged 25-49 are offered cervical screening—a pap smear test—every three years through their doctor. Keep your checks up-to-date.

- Consider having a flu shot each fall.

- Check your Body Mass Index (BMI) to make sure that your weight falls in the right range for your height. See https://www.cdc.gov/healthyweight/assessing/index.html

- Check breasts or testicles once a month. Look at them in the mirror and feel them to monitor any changes. Changes, including lumps, can occur for many reasons and the vast majority of lumps are not cancerous. However, you should always have any changes checked out.

LIFE ADMIN AND ETIQUETTE

Let this section be your guide to getting your life sorted out, being the best host and the guest everyone wants to invite.

TELL WHEN YOU CHANGE ADDRESS

As well as telling your family and friends, tell your:

- Employer, or IRS (the tax office) if you're self-employed or working from home.

- Utility companies: electricity, water, gas.

- Cable and satellite TV providers and TV licenser.

- Broadband, Wi-Fi, mobile phone and landline suppliers.

- Doctor, dentist, optician.

- Bank, credit card company, building society.

- Mortgage, insurance and pension companies.

- Federal, state, and local tax revenue agencies, as well as local governments responsible for parking permits, benefits, etc.

- Investment companies.

- Accountant, solicitor, social worker.

- DMV, breakdown recovery provider.

- Gym and membership clubs, including school and university alumni associations.

- Store and airline loyalty schemes and online shopping retailers.

- The new occupants of your former address.

For a fee you can ask the Post Office to redirect your mail to your new address for three, six or 12 months.

WRITE A RESUME

Your resume is a summary of your education, work experience and skills. It should be no longer than two pages, unless you are a medic or academic with considerable experience to show.

Start with your name, address and contact details, then a short profile summary of yourself, for example:

I am an English graduate with experience in PR and marketing. As a natural communicator, I can interact with clients effectively and I can create and deliver campaigns that meet clients' business objectives. I am keen to develop my management and people skills to new heights.

A traditional resume follows reverse chronological order, showing your most recent work positions first, then your education achievements, followed by skills and additional attainments such as proficiency in a foreign language or software programs. Finally, add your interests or hobbies if there's space. If you've just left further education, list your academic background and achievements first and then any work experience. Always include dates.

Present details of your responsibilities and achievements in previous jobs in a succinct and compelling way. Where possible, link your interests to demonstrate your fitness for the job. For instance: if you're applying for a job in fashion, reference your styling blog.

Format your information so it is easy to read and make use of bold type for headings and bullet points.

Rather than writing just one resume, tailor the content to highlight your suitability for each job you apply for.

HOW TO
WRITE A LETTER

Sometimes only a formal letter will do. Whether it's typed or handwritten, the usual layout is set out in this example:

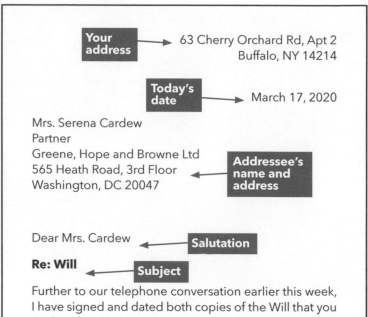

Your address → 63 Cherry Orchard Rd, Apt 2
Buffalo, NY 14214

Today's date → March 17, 2020

Mrs. Serena Cardew
Partner
Greene, Hope and Browne Ltd
565 Heath Road, 3rd Floor ← **Addressee's name and address**
Washington, DC 20047

Dear Mrs. Cardew ← **Salutation**

Re: Will ← **Subject**

Further to our telephone conversation earlier this week, I have signed and dated both copies of the Will that you drafted for me, and it has also been signed by the two witnesses as required. I enclose one original copy with this letter to you for you to keep in safe custody on my behalf as agreed.

Also attached is the completed direct debit form that

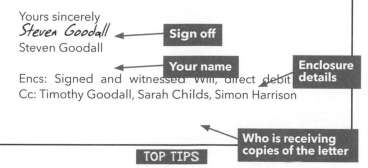

you sent me to set up the annual safe custody charge of $65 per annum.

As you suggested, I have made my named executors aware that you have custody of a copy in the event of my demise.

Thank you for organizing this for me, and I have made a note to review my Will should my personal circumstances, or my wishes, change.

Yours sincerely

Steven Goodall ← **Sign off**

Steven Goodall

← **Your name**

Encs: Signed and witnessed Will, direct debit **Enclosure details**

Cc: Timothy Goodall, Sarah Childs, Simon Harrison

← **Who is receiving copies of the letter**

TOP TIPS

- Keep the body of your letter as short as possible and to the point. Check that you have stated what action, if any, is required by the recipient.

- Put "Dear Sir/Dear Madam" as the salutation if you don't know the name of the recipient and match it with "Yours faithfully" as your sign off. Keep "Yours sincerely" for when you do know the name of the addressee.

- Read your letter over again before you send it to review it for clarity, as well as grammar and spelling errors. Be sure that you've covered all the information pertinent to the recipient and keep a copy for yourself.

APPLY FOR A JOB/ WRITE A COVER LETTER

While many jobs these days involve online applications, it is still a common requirement to send your resume and a cover letter or email.

For the letter, follow the rules for formal letter writing and always quote the job reference in the header to clarify which job you are applying for. The letter needn't be long and mustn't exceed a single sheet of paper, so don't ramble. It needs to supplement your resume by focusing on why you want the job principally, as well as your suitability and enthusiasm for the role. Find a way to reference a positive fact about the company so it shows you're up-to-date about what it does and where it is heading.

If you're not confident about spelling or grammar, ask a family member or friend to read the letter before you send it off. If you are applying online or by email, save your letter as a PDF as any computer can view this file format.

If you are writing on spec to see if a company you'd like to work for has a vacancy, do your research on the organization. Look up who you should address the letter to and address them by name, if possible. This will help your letter stand out!

It's rare to be asked to apply in writing. Should this be the case, write neatly and legibly using a good pen and simple writing paper. Choose an envelope big enough to accommodate your resume without overfolding it.

HOW TO
ACE AN INTERVIEW

Whether you're doing your interview online or face-to-face, treat it seriously and do your research beforehand. Practice delivering some answers before the interview. Be clear on why the organization needs you and how you can add value.

If you are being interviewed online, set up your device with a plain background behind you and in a quiet room where there will be no interruptions. Position the camera so you can be seen from the waist up. Test all aspects of your tech before the interview. Make eye contact with the camera, sit up straight and don't talk too fast.

Dress in the style appropriate for the company or organisation you hope to join. If you're doing a face-to-face interview, arrive early and don't be spotted checking out your phone screen while you're waiting to be called in. Ensure it's switched off before you arrive.

Group interviews are often conducted to see how you might work with others as a team. Make sure you listen to what's going on and that you are seen to say something. Dilemmas may be posed to test how you might handle a client or customer query; your approach to the issue might be more important than knowing the "right" solution.

Try to appear relaxed in a one-to-one interview, without coming across as nonchalant. Aim to make at least 50 percent of the contribution to the dialogue. Sell yourself and your talents well but know when to stop.

HOW TO
HAGGLE IN SHOPS OR MARKETS

Most shops have set prices and if you are dealing with general sales staff they probably won't have the authority to offer discounts, unless you are buying in high volume or spending a great deal of money. However, there are exceptions: for example, on large price-tag items like cars, fitted kitchens, furniture and major appliances, where there is an expectation of discounts or extras.

It's always worth asking for a deal. Say to a sales assistant that you're interested in buying a particular bed and ask if a mattress protector or a couple of pillows can be thrown in, too.

Owner-managers of independent shops may be more willing to offer discounts to regular shoppers, or if you are seen to be indecisive about buying three or more high-price items. Towards the end of a sales period you may be able to secure an extra percentage discount on an item if the shop is keen to clear stock.

Markets are better hunting grounds for hagglers looking to lower the asking price. In many countries haggling at market stalls is expected. Remember: only haggle if you are serious about buying. Think about what price you are prepared to pay; between counter offers this should end up around midway between the seller's proposed price and your lowest starting offer. Be prepared to walk away if you can't agree a price.

Do be realistic about when you can push for money off purchases in stores and remember that it pays to be polite when asking.

NEGOTIATE A PAY RAISE

Preparation is all that's needed to give you the confidence to succeed in a face-to-face negotiation. So do your research first:

- Check what the going rate is for similar positions elsewhere and assess what you're worth. Based on your findings, choose a figure that would satisfy you and ask for a bit more so there is room to maneuver.

- Think when you would like your new rate to start so you can bring this into your negotiation as necessary.

- Request a formal meeting with your boss. Try to avoid a time when they might be extremely busy or stressed.

- Make a case for why you think you should be paid more— for example, increased responsibilty, good performance, increased input or length of time on the same salary.

- Be prepared to offer something else of value to your current role to secure your raise.

- Never cite someone else's higher salary in your company as a reason for why you think you should be paid more, even if they are newer or more junior than you. Your employer will not be impressed that this is public knowledge and it is up to them to pay what they like.

- Plan a strategy, should you meet with resistance. Don't threaten to leave unless you are serious; your resignation might be accepted. Do check when you can ask again and consider if there's a beneficial training course you could ask the company to pay for that you could attend in the meantime.

MANAGE YOUR FINANCES

To manage and plan your spending, first work out a budget. Record your income and what you spend each month. For example:

- **Recurring monthly payments:** Rent/mortgage, utilities, taxes, pension, loans.

- **Daily and general expenses:** Travel, food, fuel.

- **Extras:** Entertainment and leisure, vacations, Christmas, parties, unforeseen bills.

- **Savings:** Money for future plans and contingency for some of the extras.

Being aware of what you're spending makes it easier to work out what to trim. For example, cutting back on take-out and coffee shop treats could fund a fantastic vacation.

Insure against the worst happening: it can save you from possible mega bills if it does.

Try to only have one credit card and put on it only what you can afford to pay off each month in full. The credit facility can be a lifeline in emergencies, but not if your card is maxed out.

Download any of the well-rated apps available to manage your own spending, or to divvy up expenditure with others.

Start saving for your pension as soon as possible—doing this as a regular drip-feed of savings from your twenties onwards will have a dramatically better outcome than starting in your thirties. Financial wizards estimate that you need to put aside 12.5 percent of your salary for 40 years before you retire to build up a safe pension pot. Part-time work in later life is a developing trend, but this depends on continued good health and the ability to secure that employment.

PAY OFF DEBT

Borrowings for mortgages, student loans or loans for specific items are positive, since they reward you with the gain of a home, a degree, or a useful or desired purchase—as long as you can afford the payments. However, you're in the danger zone if you're running up an overdraft without having enough income to clear it. Unless it's tackled, debt can set you back for years due to high interest charges; it may also give you lower credit scores.

A firm action plan is required:

- Calculate what you owe to whom. Don't leave anything out.

- Draw up a budget including a schedule for repaying your debts. Prioritize: items such as mortgages, utilities and taxes come first.

- Pay off as much as you can. If you only make the minimum monthly payments it will take you considerably longer to make any headway with the overall sum.

- Don't borrow any more money or incur any additional debts until you've repaid your existing ones.

- Curb your spending by cutting up your credit and store cards, or giving them to someone you trust for safekeeping. Take a set sum of cash out of your bank account once a week and live off that only.

- Switch to a cheaper credit card or loan provider to keep the interest from racking up on your current debt. Some offer 0 percent interest for an initial period. Note when the 0 percent period is up and switch again. Check for balance transfer fees and annual charges.

HOW TO

UNDERSTAND EMAIL ETIQUETTE

- Clarify the topic concisely in the subject line and update it if the discussion changes.

- Never put anything in an email that you wouldn't say in public.

- Use good English—no slang, text abbreviations, emojis or inappropriate exclamation marks. Re-read your email before you send it. Check for typos or missing attachments.

- Stay formal until you know your recipient better. "Dear" can become "Hello" or "Hi" over time. Likewise, stick with "Kind regards" or "Regards"—"Best wishes" comes later.

- Have a proper email signature set-up which includes your name, title and full contact details.

- Respond to all points raised by the sender. Be clear on what the next actions should be.

- Thank recipients if they've done something helpful; thank them in advance for something you're asking them to do.

- Send large or numerous attachments via a file transfer system and notify the recipient.

- Don't fire off a reply when you are angry. Wait until your emotions are under control.

- Protect people's privacy when emailing groups by hiding their email addresses in a "bcc" box.

- Pick up the phone, make a Skype call or FaceTime. Sometimes issues need discussion that's better handled by a conversation. Follow up with an email once an action has been agreed.

PROTECT YOUR HOME COMPUTER

MALWARE

Sophisticated malware designed to harvest your financial details and passwords is concealed in phishing emails and malicious web links. If you suspect you've been attacked, disconnect from the Wi-Fi and use another computer to change all your passwords.

Running an anti-virus program can protect against ransomware, which can take over your computer and demands payment to restore your files.

BACK UP YOUR FILES

Keep your software up-to-date and back up your files, so all is not lost under any circumstances.

All your phone contacts should be shared to your PC or laptop and backed-up regularly, or you could lose the lot. Some linked devices will do this automatically. Otherwise, back up manually via a cable connection.

Use a routine back-up method that's quick to do as you're more likely to stick with it—for instance, using an external hard-drive to copy your files to. Cloud-based services have the added advantage of keeping files safe from fire, theft and computer failures as all copies are stored away from your home. Save your work as you go straight to the cloud. Services tend to be free for basic storage capacity and you can install your chosen provider on all your devices, enabling changes to your files or documents to be synced across them all. Subscription charges apply for large amounts of data.

MANAGE YOUR TIME

Procrastination is your enemy! Vow to start early in the day to achieve more and crack on.

Make a "To do" list of tasks to be accomplished. Date your list and refresh it periodically; write it by hand if you're motivated by seeing how many items you have completed. Put a dash against items that can't be finished until others have been responded to, to show yourself some progress, and break down big tasks with sub-entries to tick off as you work through them.

Each day, tackle the two or three most important tasks first. Focus on these crucial jobs without distraction and tick them off your list. You'll have done what's essential and feel good that your load has been lightened.

Set yourself a target time limit for completing tasks—for instance, doing a set amount of work before lunch. Be realistic about how long it will take you to do a task and don't beat yourself up if it was more complex than it first appeared. Don't let unimportant details in the task ambush your time. The key to completion is to not let unnecessary distractions eat away at your time, so keep cell phones out of sight and unrelated browser windows shut until you're done.

Keeping a separate "To do" list for personal things that need to be done or remembered, or that you would like to do, can also help with time management in your private life.

BE A GOOD HOST

WEEKEND AND OVERNIGHT GUESTS

Provide your guests with clean bedding, plenty of pillows and fluffy towels, a spare blanket in cold weather, water glasses and a carafe of fresh water. Check the bedside lights work, leave some light bedside reading and give them some space to hang or store clothes. A small jug of flowers in the bedroom can be welcoming. Check there's soap and toilet paper in the bathroom.

Make life easy for everyone by printing out the Wi-Fi code, how the house alarm works and any parking regulations before your guests arrive. Tell them what your schedule is, if you're working or need to do everyday things while they are around. Help them with local knowledge if they're planning some sightseeing without you and lend them a spare set of keys. Offer your guests food and drink or show them how to help themselves.

PARTY AND MEAL GUESTS

- Cook something you already know how to do to sidestep culinary disasters and food arriving late at the table. In fact, make sure there is plenty to eat and drink and you can't go far wrong!

- Give your guests a drink on arrival and something to nibble at before the meal.

- Create a mellow playlist to give a relaxed ambience during a supper party and a lively one for dance parties.

- Resolve to do the bulk of the clearing up the next day so everyone can enjoy the evening.

BE A GOOD WEEKEND GUEST

- Ask your host when they would prefer you to arrive. Even if they're laid back it's considerate to clarify, for instance, whether you will arrive in time for Friday night supper, or fully-fed afterwards.

- Arrive with a gift. Thoughtful trumps extravagant! Fine toiletries, chocolates, wine, flowers or a houseplant are all good standbys; well-chosen books, DVDs and seasonal foods can go down well, too.

- Ask what you need to bring. Country walking gear? Smart clothes for a dinner? Swimming kit and a towel? Don't forget to pack your PJs or other night attire as well.

- Be prepared to join in with games and activities. No one's likely to force you onto a horse, or on a long hike, but you could drive to meet up with your host or fellow guests at the bar.

- Take your cue from your host. Limit lounging in bed for hours, unless encouraged to do so. Sitting around in your nightwear eating breakfast while lunch prep is in full swing is deemed rude in certain households.

- Do offer to help. Unless you're in a formal environment with staff, your offer will be appreciated. Helping in the kitchen, laying the table, or clearing away afterwards can ensure that you are asked to stay again.

- Don't outstay your welcome. Be prepared to disappear after Sunday lunch unless you are genuinely pressed to stay longer.

- Ask whether you should remake or strip the bed before you go.

HOW TO
SET A TABLE

Although you may not have to lay a table for a formal dinner too often, it helps to know the layout when attending or helping at such an event.

This diagram shows the most commonly used items and their placement. The cutlery is always placed in the order of use for each course, starting on the outside, with forks on the left, knives on the right and the dessert spoon and fork above the place setting. If you're using a soup spoon it should always be laid on the same side as the knives. Knife blades point inwards towards the center.

Table laying at home is a simplified version of this—less formal and with fewer courses.

Add salt, pepper and other condiments to the table to suit the meal, plus spoons to serve them with. Heatproof mats and sufficient serving spoons need laying out if you're dishing up at the table or letting others help themselves.

Steak knives with serrated blades can also be handy to have for easy slicing on the plate.

DESSERT SPOON

DESSERT FORK

FISH FORK

FISH KNIFE

MEAT FORK

SALAD FORK

SALAD KNIFE

MEAT KNIFE

HOW TO
TIE A TIE

Not everyone's school uniform included a tie. Nevertheless, at some stage you might need to know how to tie one for work, a formal occasion or even for fancy dress!

If you want to be taken seriously, there'll be no lazy pulling-over-your-head-in-one-piece stuff. Start from scratch every time for a knot that sits well and tie ends that stay in place.

1 Turn up your collar. Put the tie round your neck with the left side much shorter than the right.

2 Hold the left side in one hand and with the other, wrap the long side round the short.

3 Repeat step 2.

4 Tuck the rest of the long side under and feed it up through the back of the "V" shape.

5 Feed the long end down and into the front loop of the knot. Smooth out any bunching of the sides immediately under the knot.

6 Hold onto the short end with one hand and hold the knot with the other hand to tighten and adjust it until it sits snugly under where the wings of your collar meet. Turn your collar down. Tidy the short end of your tie away from sight behind the long end.

TIE A BOW TIE

Look in the mirror and follow these steps.

1 Turn up your collar and drape the tie round your neck. The left side should be about an inch longer than the right. Cross the left side over the right side.

2 Tie a single knot and hold the longer length of tie up straight.

3 Fold the shorter end into a bow across your top shirt button and hold in place.

4 Let the straight end of the tie drop so you have T-shape. Hold the junction of the T-shape to secure all the layers of fabric together. Pinch the dangling length of tie in half at its widest point to form the second part of the bow.

5 Take it up and feed it through the knot behind the top of the T.

6 Pull the looped ends to tighten. Tidy and straighten as necessary. Turn your collar down.

WRITE A THANK-YOU NOTE

A thank-you note needn't be long, but a promptly sent handwritten one goes down well—particularly with the older generation. With your contemporaries, you may get away with a text message or an email, but a handwritten note shows more consideration.

A friend might ask you to celebrate a milestone birthday, join them on vacation or invite you to their wedding, but if it's their parents who are paying it's to them that thanks are due.

If you don't possess headed paper or cards, a note card will do fine. Choose your best pen—black or blue ink is preferable—write your address in the top right-hand corner, put the date underneath and add the salutation on the left-hand side.

If witty words don't come naturally to you, plan what you are going to write beforehand. Start by thanking the recipient—for the invite or the present in question—and then reference memorable highlights. For example: the host's generosity; how much you enjoyed yourself/ liked your present; the quality of the food/wine/entertainment/ setting/speeches; and who you enjoyed meeting. Don't stint on complimentary adjectives; they may feel a little over the top when putting pen to paper but it will give the recipient a glow of pleasure to read them. Expand with your hope to see them soon, a return invitation or good wishes for a forthcoming event in their lives.

Sign off with "Yours sincerely", "Best wishes" or "Love", as appropriate, before your name.

SEND A FORMAL INVITATION

Printed invitations are still considered desirable for formal parties and weddings. The wording can vary from relatively informal— "John and Sue invite you for drinks at home"—to highly formal—"Mr. and Mrs. John Bloggs request the pleasure of your company at the marriage of their daughter, Sarah Jane, to Mr. William James Smith".

The key facts to include are:

- Type of event: Drinks, birthday party, wedding, anniversary and so forth.
- Who's hosting the celebration and who it is for, if there's a difference.
- The start time, date and venue in full and the dress code.
- RSVP: Whom to reply to, how to reply and by when.
- Catering details: For example, "drinks and canapés".
- The time the event is due to draw to a close, if appropriate.

Your printer will have a stock of examples for you to follow and can advise on paper weight, fonts and embellishment if desired.

Allow time for printing and aim to post out the invitations at least six weeks before the event to give the best chance of your guests being available to attend.

Write the name of your guest(s) in full, including titles, in ink in the top left-hand corner if there is no space provided on the invitation for this. Include a reply card with a stamped, self-addressed envelope if you wish, along with any maps, lists of accommodation or other details, as appropriate.

ANSWER A FORMAL INVITATION

Some formal invitations include reply cards. If so, fill in the blanks as appropriate and return.

Otherwise reply on writing paper, showing your address at the top. Include the name of your "guest" or "partner" in your reply if the invitation extends beyond just you.

The conventional way to reply follows this formula:

Miss Sarah Smith thanks Mrs. Nigel Johnson for her kind invitation to drinks and dinner on Friday July 24, which she accepts with great pleasure/which she much regrets being unable to accept.

For wedding invitations, address the hostess on the front of the envelope when you reply.

The reply customarily mirrors the wording of the invitation:

Mr. Simon Brown thanks Mr. and Mrs. John Bloggs for the kind invitation to the marriage of their daughter, Sarah Jane, to Mr. William James Smith at St. Peter's Church, Northington, on Saturday April 16 at 2 p.m. and afterwards at Little Thorpe House and is delighted to accept/regrets that he is unable to accept.

Nowadays, many hosts like to send out "save the date" email notifications in advance of a formal invitation. These should be replied to promptly using the same wording as above, but in the first person. Unless the formal invitation requests a follow-up RSVP, then the job is done.

MAKE A GOOD IMPRESSION AT A FORMAL DINNER OR EVENT

Observe the dress code specified on the invitation. Clean, shiny shoes, a crisp shirt and tie and a well-pressed suit show a man who cares about his appearance; for women at a smart wedding it is conventional not to wear black or white, show too much bare skin during the church service or to outshine the bride.

Unless previously agreed with your host, arrive at the time specified on the invitation. This is particularly important for a sit-down dinner or a church service.

At the dinner table, stand until bidden to sit. Once in your seat, unfold your table napkin and place it on your lap. Always wait for your hostess to start eating before you do. This is also helpful if you are unsure about how to eat something unfamiliar, or what cutlery to use and when.

Talk to the person on your left during the first course, then to the person on your right during the main course. This way, no one is left out of a conversation.

If the waiting staff are not in constant attendance, ensure that you offer wine, water, condiments and any other item your neighbor might be short of, or that is out of reach, before you serve yourself. Hold serving dishes for them while they help themselves.

Don't overindulge!

GIVE A TOAST

Although the host traditionally proposes the first toast on most formal occasions, when friends gather informally, as a guest you can toast your host to thank them for their hospitality and any other reason you wish—friendship, long life, love, congratulations, good fortune or happiness.

Toasts should not be confused with speeches; they should be kept short and to the point.

Before leading the toast at a semi-formal occasion, check that the guests' glasses and your own have been charged before commencing. Attract everyone's attention by standing, or sitting yourself in a prominent place.

Briefly introduce yourself and the reason for the gathering. Go on to express a goodwill wish towards the future of the person(s) concerned—for example, "May you be ever light of heart and calm of mind." Ask the assembly to raise their glasses by raising your own glass while saying, "To [name of person/subject of toast]." They should respond by repeating your toast. Take a sip from your glass which will allow them to follow your example.

If all around you are seated, ask them to, "Please stand and raise your glasses to…" Official toastmasters at formal events will use more flowery language: "Lords, ladies and gentlemen, please be upstanding for…" Note that at a wedding reception, etiquette dictates that it's the best man's job to propose the first toast.

WHISTLE WITH YOUR FINGERS

It will take a bit of practice to produce more than a splutter so be prepared to experiment until you find your personal sweet spot to achieve an ear-splitting whistle. Don't give up and you'll get there in the end.

Choose the finger combination that feels the most natural to you. Most people plump for one of the following:

- Forming a closed "C" shape with the thumb and forefinger of one hand.

- Making an "A" frame shape with the index finger of each hand.

- Both the index and middle finger of each hand.

The technique is the same for any of these.

Start with clean hands. Cover your bottom set of teeth with your bottom lip. The harder you press your lip down into your teeth, the louder your whistle will be. With your chosen finger shape, push down on your lip with the first joint of your digits. Curl your tongue back and use your fingers to keep it there.

Take a deep breath to fill up your lungs with air and close your lips together. Exhale as fast as you can through the gap between your fingers.

Keep practicing until you achieve a good result. Take a break if you feel dizzy from too many in-and-out exhalations. Adjust the position of your fingers, lips, mouth and tongue until you find what works for you.

BE A GOOD HOUSEMATE OR NEIGHBOR

- Pay your share of agreed bills on time, including food and household items.

- Don't space-invade: keep common areas tidy, know when to retreat to your room and don't borrow personal items without asking.

- Keep sinks, basins, toilets, and baths clean for the next person.

- Don't use the last of something without replacing it: milk, toilet roll and so forth.

- Got some of next door's mail? Make sure you give it to them; missed mail could have serious consequences for the recipients.

- Give any neighbors a few days' notice if you are planning a loud or large party.

- In the summer months, keep music, radio and TV noise down if you have windows open.

- Keep party noise to weekends and not beyond midnight. If you want to carry on, turn any music down, keep windows and doors shut or go clubbing instead. Loud mobile phone calls in the yard are a no-no, too.

- Keep your household waste in trash cans with the lids firmly on. No one wants to see or smell your rubbish and loose trash bags will be ripped open by local wildlife and pets.

- Keep yards tidy and weed-free—a landlord's requirement if you are renting.

THE ART OF GOOD CONVERSATION

"Talk is cheap," they say. Make what you say and how you say it count with these pearls of wisdom.

HOW TO

MAKE SMALL TALK

Arrive early to parties and functions. Why? Because it is easier to find another person on their own in the early stages of a gathering and being one of the first few lessens the chance of everyone already talking in groups when you turn up. However, if you've had to come later, target a small group to join that's left a gap in its circle.

Although deep down we are conditioned to think that small talk is trivial, we need to use it to connect with others. Small talk is the basis on which more authentic conversations grow.

When you walk into an event, you might be apprehensive. You won't be alone in this. By reaching out to converse with others you can put both them and yourself at ease.

An observation about anything in the room can be all that is needed as an ice-breaker. For example, "Wow! These flower arrangements are lavish!" You haven't given away what you think about the flowers or criticized the host's choice of flora; you've shown yourself to be friendly and open. You could follow it up with, "I wish I knew more about flowers. Do you know what those big ones in the center are?" Allowing the other person to display their knowledge is a good starter and even if they know as little about flowers as you, you have discovered common ground.

Asking questions is another way to start a conversation. The wedding classic is, "Do you know the bride or the groom?" Other openers are, "How do you know our hosts?" or "Where are you from?" Listen to the answers for clues about where to go next with the conversation and bring out your inner journalist! When the other person names their hometown, ask them what it's like to live there or what led them to be there. Asking their opinion is another technique—for example, "What did you think of that course module?" When you are asked about yourself resist monosyllabic answers, which are conversation killers. Offer conversation bait instead. If the other person asks, "What have you been up to today?", instead of responding with "Nothing exciting" say something like, "I've been busy packing up my apartment"–this can give them a steer on what to ask you next.

Keep off contentious subjects like politics and religion. Learn at least one new fact a day from a reliable source and you'll be amazed at how often these can be used as conversation topics. Broadening your knowledge of the world pays off on these occasions.

Striking up conversations with strangers takes practice. Don't be put off by the odd disaster. You'll become adept at it before you know it!

CONVERSE WITH A YOUNGER PERSON

Here's a trick for starting interaction with little children to whom you've just been introduced. Resist making direct eye contact. Sit down on the floor a short distance away and start to be busy with an activity, within their line of sight. Play intently with one of the child's toys, have a pretend conversation with a teddy or tussle a ball in the jaws of a friendly dog. Most children will start to be intrigued. Carry on and give the child an occasional smile. Before long, even the shyest child will want to join in. The opportunity to talk about what you're doing, or their favorite thing, will soon follow.

Older children can be coaxed into conversation by focusing on what they like—best TV shows, favored apps, closest friends, sports followed, favorite foods and pets are all good bets.

Young teens can feel shy around older teenagers. You may recall feeling overshadowed by the seeming glamour and confidence of those further up the developmental chain. If you are now in this position, a genuine interest in them and their opinions can make them shine. Develop a rapport with them by drawing them out to talk about their passions.

Older teenagers tend to be easier to talk with and there is plenty to talk about: their plans for college, university, work experience and travel. Some may already be working or be on an apprentice scheme. Conversation gambits can therefore be naturally more varied.

END A CONVERSATION

If your listener is getting fidgety and distracted while you're talking, it could be a sign you've stayed on one subject for too long. It's either time to stop dominating the conversation or to move on and talk to someone else.

Should the boot be on the other foot, wait for a pause and aim to wrap up the conversation on an upbeat note and with a smile. For instance, "I'm glad to hear your family is doing so well, Liz. Good luck with the new baby," as you retreat.

If you're trapped by a windbag, the chances are you both have empty glasses. Offer to go and fetch you both a refill. When you return, hand over the glass as you pass by with a breezy, "Good to meet you." By this time, they may have found a new victim to latch on to.

If they refuse a fresh drink, you are free to seek one yourself, saying, "I really enjoyed meeting you." Here are some other get-outs: "Have you spotted the cloakroom?" "Do you know Harry?" as you introduce them to each other and slide away. "So sorry to desert you but I have to catch Sally before she leaves." "I haven't said hello to our hosts yet, I'd better go and do that now." "I've left something in my coat pocket, do you mind if I get it while I remember?" "I need some fresh air; would you please excuse me?"

HOW TO

SAY, "I'M SORRY"

Saying "sorry" is a challenging but inevitable part of life. Here are some tips to make saying that little word a bit easier.

Say sorry whenever it is warranted. It can often go a long way to mollifying an increasingly tense situation.

Confess when you've done the wrong thing. Don't think that an apology demeans you in any way; in fact, not apologizing is much more likely to do so. Saying "I'm really sorry" doesn't automatically lead to forgiveness when you have hurt someone or done something wrong; it's a step in the right direction though.

Mean what you say. Do resist saying "I'm sorry" in a sarcastic tone, it tells the other person you think they are unnecessarily touchy and that they are wrong to expect any kind of apology. Instead, aim to be sincere.

If the situation that required the apology is more serious, you may need a strategy for moving forward in a positive way with the person or people concerned. Ask if there is anything you can do to make it up to the other person. Do you need to state that you will modify your behavior or promise not to let a similar situation occur in future? This is part of reassuring others that you are genuine in your intentions not to repeat the same mistake.

HOW TO

SAY, "THANK YOU"

"Thank you" is one of the most powerful phrases in your lexicon. Never neglect to say it frequently as an act of appreciation for what others have done for you, even on the smallest scale. Express your thanks on notepaper, or in the form of a tangible gift if appropriate, and you will build a reputation for being considerate and kind. Always be sincere when you offer thanks.

Show thanks and gratitude by text or email when work colleagues, clients and comparative strangers have helped you, or if you are asking for their time and assistance. Thank and praise your colleagues to their face, whatever level they are—not just for big pieces of project work or new business wins, but for everyday things like finding something for you, adapting an image or rewording something, or putting themselves out for you when they have a pile of other things to do. Go further when you can and tell them what a good job they have done. Watch them smile in appreciation.

It costs very little to say thank you but it makes a world of difference to others and to how others perceive you. (And don't forget that other essential—to frequently say "please"!)

HOW TO
SAY, "NO"

Are you a pushover when someone asks you to do something? Can you cope when you are asked for a favor out of your comfort zone? For example, a friend wants a loan: your mind is screaming "no" but you don't know how to sidestep the request. In this circumstance, it helps to refuse in a way that doesn't leave the friend feeling they're untrustworthy. For instance, an all-encompassing, "I've made it a rule never to lend money to friends." Explanations phrased in a way that don't sound like personal rejections are a good strategy. On some occasions, offering an alternative works well. When asked by your boss to do an additional task in the workplace that's not going to fit your workload, say, for instance, "Project X is what I'm working on now, can this wait until afterwards, or do you want me to reprioritize?" They might not have remembered you have so much to do and you are not refusing to help. A friend might ask, "Can I bring my new girlfriend round to dinner, too?" If this doesn't suit say, "I've already got as many as I can manage coming but why don't we arrange a night out together, so I can meet her?" Being able to say "no" is one of the most valuable skills you can learn. It will make sure you don't take on too much, keep you from feeling resentful and allow you to prioritize what's important in your life.

HOW TO
FORGIVE

Forgiveness is about letting the emotional heat of the wrong done against you subside, gradually accepting what has happened and finding a way to live with it, then moving on with your life. This pertains to whether it is a person that has done something hurtful, or if you've experienced life-changing circumstances.

It is entirely up to you whether you are willing to forgive a hurt or terrible wrongdoing against you; in deeply hurtful, abusive or tragic situations it may be impossible to ever forgive.

Forgiveness doesn't mean you must tell the other person that you forgive them, although you can if you are ready to do so. Forgiving someone also doesn't mean that they have to be part of your life any more. You're in control of that.

You need to give yourself time to process your feelings about an incident before you can park any upset or anger. However, be aware of yourself—holding on to bitterness can end up being destructive for you. Remember: harboring a grudge debilitates you rather than the other person.

Think about why the incident happened, why the other person behaved as they did or how conditions came about to put you in an awful position. Is there anything that you might have done wrong? Can you see why the other person conducted themselves as they did? This, and no longer obsessing about how put upon you feel, can help take you to the point of forgiveness and acceptance.

ASK FOR HELP

There is no weakness in asking for help. On the contrary, the weakness is in thinking you know the answer to everything.

We all need help to thrive, accomplish and develop. This often includes asking for help from others to fill in gaps in our own knowledge or understanding, or for advice in solving a dilemma. Other people can often point us in the right direction, even if they can't provide a direct answer.

You might be surprised to find that people often want to help you, as it makes them feel good and useful. Phrase your request in a flattering way to unlock this instinct. You might say, "I'm a bit stuck and I know you're just the right person to help me with this" or "Please may I ask for your advice?" There may be occasions when you are physically ill and need help. Your friends and family will undoubtedly ask if you need help, but to turn the kind offers into actual action requires you to be specific about what sort of help you need—for example, buying and preparing food, picking up medication, changing bed linen or providing transportation. Ask your willing helpers to take on an errand. Match the task to the person's strengths and your comfort level if the task is an intimate one. Resist micromanaging how it's done and always thank your helpers, no matter how small their contribution.

GIVE A COMPLIMENT

Complimenting others should figure in your armory of social skills. It's an excellent way to show appreciation and give praise where it is due.

TOP TIPS

- Remember to do it, but be mindful not to overdo it or be too fulsome in your offer of praise—you don't want to make the other person uncomfortable.

- Charm others with compliments but always be genuine and sincere.

- Compliment people on specifics about their personal taste and skills, such as their clothing, interior decorating, cooking or singing. Saying something rewarding about another's personality trait will be regarded as special but you need to know the person well for this.

- Be mindful of paying compliments to someone you are making a sales pitch to—you are more likely to put them on their guard.

- Never underestimate how motivating praise can be, in or out of the workplace. A compliment paid on a small thing well-done can be just as important as acclaim for a big project—sometimes it's more important. Encouragement at just the right moment can boost a flagging morale or buy you willingness from someone else to go the extra mile when you need a favor.

- If you hear good things about a person when they're not present from a third party, do pass it on and watch them smile.

- Finally, remember: a backhanded compliment isn't a compliment; it's a snide remark.

ACCEPT A COMPLIMENT

Compliments are lovely to receive. They are a measure of being noticed by others for something positive about ourselves.

It's often a surprise when we receive a compliment from others and therefore it is easy to be flummoxed on the occasion it happens. A natural default is to look embarrassed and to either mumble a self-deprecating comment, or deny what is being said to us. Really, this is false modesty and unintentionally takes away from the kindness intended by the person giving the compliment. The other person has shown generosity of spirit in offering the compliment in the first place and to deflect their kind words is not polite. It can imply that their compliment is not sincere or that their judgement is poor.

The trick is to not be blindsided by a well-meaning accolade and to accept it gracefully by saying, "Thank you. That is so kind of you to say so."—or words to that effect—delivered with a smile.

Do share credit when it is due to others besides yourself, by naming who else should be included when the compliment is unwittingly directed to you alone.

RESPOND TO CRITICISM

It's instinctive to default to a defensive mode when we're criticized. We can become angry, dismissive of the criticism, make an excuse or respond with a complaint about the other person.

There is value in constructive criticism, as it can help us grow or give us greater self-awareness in our dealings with friends and family. Taking what's said into account can improve your interpersonal skills and your relationships.

You may want to counter negative, or seemingly unfair, criticism with a perspective of your own. Whether criticism is positive or otherwise, here's how to deal with it graciously:

- Process what you've been told before you react. This gives you a moment to control those impulsive emotions.

- Acknowledge what has been said by paraphrasing it back. For instance, say, "So I think you are saying that…" This keeps the conversation open.

- Ask for further feedback and listen closely to what is being said without interruption. If you agree with the other person, respond by saying so and stating the action you will take to rectify the point made, then thank them for pointing out the issue.

Ask questions if you don't fully understand what is being criticized and try to pin down what that person feels can be improved in future.

Rational conversation is the best remedy for unfair criticism. Stay calm. Sometimes others might need to see things from your point of view to realize they've made a misjudgement.

ARGUE AND PERSUADE

Try out the points you want to make before you engage with the person, or people, you want to influence. Plot them as bullet points on paper. Consider how you can back them with verified facts and think about what counter points might be raised in response. Work out the strengths of your points and how to make them seem reasonable to your audience. Think of different scenarios that might make your point of view more attractive to adopt.

Be prepared to consider a compromise if it becomes necessary to concede on some aspects of your wishes. Others may have a right to have a say in the outcome, or the ultimate decision-making power.

Clarity is important when you are arguing your case, to win over others and to avoid misunderstandings. Be patient and be prepared to give the opposition a thoughtful review. That way you are more likely to win goodwill towards your recommendation. Express your concerns about opposing points of view and cite specific examples, rather than generalisations, to show why you believe these might be flawed.

Don't make it personal. Keep your reasoning about the issue in hand, not about personal behavior. Telling someone that they are always negative won't help your cause. Calmness and logic are your most valuable tools, rather than brute force or a strong display of emotion.

HOW TO

ASK SOMEONE OUT

A first date is about reaching out to learn more about the other person if they are a stranger, or an affirmation that you are taking a deeper interest in someone you already know. Perhaps your motivation is based on the desire for a physical relationship.

Just because you ask someone out once, it doesn't mean that you will spend a lifetime together. On the other hand, it might be just what you are looking for and this obviously can and does happen!

It's acceptable to text someone to suggest meeting up. Face-to-face encounters will require you to do the talking. Suggesting a decisive plan makes a good start—for example, "Would you like to come with me to the Skyline Bar on Thursday night for drinks and then to Oka for dinner?" You'll soon gauge from their reaction if you are being turned down, or whether offering an alternative night would be fine; it's better to know where you stand and take a refusal on the chin—you can't win them all. Alternatively, play safe and suggest coffee or lunch as this is a more ambiguous social setting, then fix a time and place.

Bear in mind that noisy venues and going to a movie on a first date are not the best places to choose if you want to talk.

BREAK UP WITH SOMEONE

Do as you would be done by. That means no cowardly text or email, or engineering a conversation to make them dump you. Do it face-to-face as direct contact will help the other person process why you are leaving with less room for ambiguity.

Be considerate about timing your break-up. Hang on if your other half is in exam mode, just lost their job or received other major bad news. Avoid pre-Christmas, Valentine's Day or birthday break-ups if possible, too.

Call the meeting and clarify that you want to talk about your relationship. Ideally, avoid public spaces. Think about what you want to say before you meet and how the other person might react. Be as honest as possible but not deliberately hurtful. Get to the point and be clear that you are serious about ending things to avoid giving hope that you might change your mind. Prolonged break-ups can be messy for both of you.

If you've made your point and given the chance for questions to be asked, but your ex is saying the same thing repeatedly, be firm: state that you've said what you needed to say and now it's time for you to go.

Whether you stay in touch, follow each other on social media, or still share friends is down to both of you. Sometimes it's easier to get over a relationship if all contact is severed.

PEOPLE SKILLS

Be the person that finesses those daily
interactions with others and learn how
to depend on yourself to best effect.

SHAKE HANDS

A handshake is a way to introduce yourself to another person and connect with them in a sincere and friendly way. Traditionally it's a sign that you come in peace, stemming from the days when men carried swords and daggers—a handshake created a bond of trust as it was proof that you weren't holding a weapon.

It's customary to let the person in a higher position of authority take the lead on the handshake by extending their hand out first for you to clasp in yours, firmly without exerting unnecessary pressure. The actual shaking part of the greeting should only last for a few seconds. Look to the initiator to break contact before you do.

Look the other person in the eye as you shake hands and maintain that contact as your hands part. Don't cup their elbow or touch them with your other hand in a business situation, or if you're in doubt in a social situation.

Bone-crushing grips are unwelcome and can be unpleasantly painful for those on the receiving end, particularly so for women with slender hands and be-ringed fingers. On the other hand, limp handshakes brand the giver as weak and are not ideal either. Try not to show you mind if you are presented with a sweaty palm.

When doing business abroad, check up on handshake protocol—there can be wide variations.

For instance, never offer your left hand in the Middle East; in China shake hands with the oldest people first; don't shake hands in Thailand!

HOW TO
MAKE FRIENDS

Relocating to a new city can prise you away from your home-based friends. If you are a new undergraduate, there are many opportunities to meet fellow students during Orientation Week, through joining societies, participating in sport or on your course. Taking a new job in a strange place means those ready-made chances of friendship are not available. You'll need to work harder to reach potential friends and it can take a while to build a new circle of people.

TOP TIPS

- Accept invitations from your new work colleagues, unless it's completely out of your comfort zone. They and their wider friendship group might help you to meet new companions.

- Joining a club or group, or participating in local community activities, can provide other routes to potential friendships.

- Be bold enough to strike up a conversation. Be likeable by being interested in that person. If you get on well and would like to see them again, suggest that you exchange contact details. There may be a common activity you've discovered in conversation that you can do together.

- Organize a gathering and suggest your new acquaintances bring another friend along.

- Remember that patience is often required. While instant connections can turn into lifelong friendships, with some people you have to let it bubble along, getting to know them by degrees until they are ready to deepen the acquaintance.

BE A GOOD LISTENER

- Pay attention. That includes making eye contact, not interrupting the other person and concentrating on them without being distracted by other people or things.

- Give the other person space to explain how they feel or what is troubling them without prejudice. Be tolerant of what is being said in order to be supportive, even if it's not in line with your own opinions.

- Being empathetic doesn't mean hijacking the conversation with examples of what has happened to you, particularly if they are not on the same scale. This will come across as insensitive.

- Be sympathetic. Try not to say, "I know how you feel", as it's unlikely that you do and it will sound offensive and false. Better to say, "It must be difficult to deal with your feelings about this." Don't jump in with judgements. Your ears are needed more than your views.

- Hold back on offering a solution too soon into the conversation, it can sometimes come across as a bit dismissive. Wait until you are asked for one, or it's obvious it's wanted. Sometimes to share a problem or articulate thoughts out loud is enough for the speaker.

- Respect the speaker's trust in you by considering what has been shared as confidential.

- Following up the subject later shows you care about the speaker, unless instinct tells you that it is something they would prefer not to be brought up again.

BE A GOOD FRIEND

- Be a good listener.
- Know when to offer advice and when to keep quiet.
- Be empathetic.
- Support people when they're ill, or feeling down.
- Be generous with your time; if life's too busy, ring or text.
- Remember to ask people about things that are important to them.
- Forgive their shortcomings; you have them, too. We are all only human.
- Celebrate people's successes.
- Keep their secrets.
- Remember their birthday.
- Refrain from embarrassing or upstaging others.
- Pay back money on time; don't borrow significant sums of money.
- Don't be jealous; no bitching about people behind their back.
- Clear the air if you fall out with someone; don't hold a grudge.
- Commandeering people's other friends and seeing them behind their back is a no-no.
- Don't do, or say, things that might hurt others.
- Don't steal boyfriends/girlfriends!

CONTROL YOUR TEMPER

Anger is a normal emotion. Even the most equable of us can find our temperament strained to the point where we lash out. However, it can cause problems to you and others around you if you find it difficult to keep it under control. Equally, simmering and sulking is perturbing to others around you, particularly if they are nothing to do with the source of your anger.

Anger management is not about suppressing anger, but rather finding ways of recognizing when your temper is flaring up and channelling control. The idea is that instead of blowing your top in a way you may later regret, you implement a strategy to diffuse the anger and communicate your feelings effectively.

Next time you feel anger rising, try counting to ten before you react. Give yourself a moment to assess the situation. Is your temper justified? Could you have misunderstood something? Is there another perspective to consider? Walk away for a minute or two, do some deep breathing and come back. If you're frustrated with repeat behavior from a family member, friend or colleague, present a solution.

Anger can be ingrained in your personality, but relaxation techniques and regular exercise can help reduce tension and stress levels and refresh your mind-set.

If you find yourself angry with life on a daily basis, there may be some underlying unhappiness that's causing you distress which should be addressed. Finding a level of contentment can diminish angry thoughts and negativity.

LODGE A COMPLAINT

Contact the business that you have a grievance against as soon as possible by phone, email or letter. Address your complaint to the head of the department if you can.

In the case of a purchase from a seller or an issue with a service provider, check their terms and conditions first to understand your rights. Set out your complaint in the body of an email or letter and include copies of relevant receipts, invoices and contracts. Quote any reference numbers in your correspondence. Keep a copy of your complaint and all the documents you include with it.

If you can't resolve the issue satisfactorily with the company concerned you may be able to take it to an Alternative Dispute Resolution (ADR). Companies operating in certain sectors are obliged to offer this service. Other industry sectors such as builders and vacation companies might be signed up to their relevant trade association. These types of bodies can offer independent mediation and arbitration to help settle the issue. Arbitration outcomes are final and you can't take your complaint further if you don't like the outcome.

Contacting an ombudsman is an option when you can't agree with a company over service or administrative errors.

Taking a company to the small claims court for amounts of up to about $5,000 is the ultimate action you can employ, but you will need to prove that you have tried other ways to seek reparation. The claim ceiling in other states and countries may vary.

BE A GOOD PUBLIC SPEAKER

Preparation and practice are key to success. Know your subject well, make your content engaging and your confidence will be boosted. Have a firm grasp of who your audience is, too: how deep is their knowledge of your subject matter? An understanding of this will enable you to pitch your speech at the right level.

Have structure. Start with an anecdote or joke that leads into the theme of your talk. Use examples judiciously throughout to bring alive the points you are making in listeners' heads. Finish with a summary and call to action and encourage the audience to ask questions at the end.

Plan your aids—slides, video and audio clips, props, interactive exercises, etc.—and make sure that they work before the talk. If in doubt, keep it simple. Prompts like index cards can be helpful memory joggers. A single-word reminder of a concept is more efficient than an overload of exact words.

Practice in front of a mirror or to a willing helper—or consider recording your speech. Review for the following:

- Length/timing.
- Volume and clarity of voice.
- Speed of delivery.
- Fluidity.
- Filler words to filter out, such as "um", "so" and "like".

On the day, dress professionally and leave no chance for wardrobe malfunction. Check your tech is working and connected to the Wi-Fi.

Seek friendly faces dotted around the audience and address yourself to them.

HOW TO
BE ASSERTIVE

Save yourself from being railroaded into doing things you don't want to do with these tips.

Sometimes your nearest and dearest can expect you to do everything. Take back control—try doing less and asking them to do more.

When others ask you to do them big favors, listen carefully to what they are asking and decide if it is reasonable for you to help. Suggest an alternative to you doing it, or offer a solution that suits you better. Say "no" to what you don't want to do, without giving a long justification.

Learn to resist politely when you are being pushed into doing things you don't want to do. Buy yourself time to consider the proposition and to indicate to the other person that your preferences should be considered. For example, you might say to a friend, "I'm not sure if I'm free then. I'll check and come back to you."—or to your other half you might say, "Can I have a think about that?" In a relationship, trade choices—say you'll go to a concert, festival, play or film with your partner because you know they really want to, but you would like to choose next time.

If someone has lost their phone, glasses, wallet, bag, or whatever: no need to act the guilty party if their disappearance was nothing to do with you. Say, "They must be where you last had them. What about in your coat pocket? Your bag? Down the side of the sofa? Would you like me to help look?"

HOW TO
REMEMBER NAMES

Ever been introduced to someone who doesn't look like their name? You've been told she's called Anna and your focus is lost as you decide they look like more like a Sandy. Suddenly, you can't remember what they're really called because you've lost concentration.

Train your brain to cope with remembering names as it makes people feel valued–plus it's rude if you come out with the wrong name and makes you appear rather foolish.

Start by making sure that you listen; if you're busy thinking of what you are going to say next, you're not listening.

Resolve to concentrate hard to hear a name when you are next introduced to someone and repeat their name back to them as you greet them while you look them in the eye. Commit the name to memory. Build up your technique so you can cope with trickier group introductions.

Find a way that works for you to retain the name. This can be by referencing the person's name in the subsequent conversation, or finding a visual or linguistic association. For example, picture in your head another Anna you know–a friend, relative or celebrity. Try a mnemonic for complicated names, so Kim Kardashian might become "Kim dashes to the car with Ian". Maybe you can remember a physical feature better to make the connection, or fix upon an item of clothing.

After a party or a business event, try to review who you have met and recall their names again.

READ BODY LANGUAGE

Interpreting body language comes instinctively to many and we even begin to pick up on overt movements and postures from babyhood. Some signs are obvious, some are not; some movements could be defensive or a warning for you to change your behavior, or they could be movements to put you at your ease. Here are some of the most common:

- **Leaning away from you:** You're invading their space, or either of you could have bad breath.

- **Arms crossed or folded across the body:** A defensive posture, a sign of discomfort, entrenchment—or your companion could simply be cold!

- **Splayed legs when seated:** A confident, relaxed person. Could be a little too casual if serious issues are being discussed.

- **Fidgeting or thumb twiddling:** Can be a sign of impatience or wishing to be somewhere else.

- **Hand on hip and one foot forward when standing:** A positive position indicating a good mood.

- **Fingering neck or collar:** Nervousness, doubt, insecurity.

- **Crossed legs when seated:** This person is comfortable and receptive.

- **Arms behind the back when standing:** Says "keep your distance" when a hand is not proffered in greeting. Alternatively, it can indicate the person is feeling relaxed and confident.

NETWORK

It's important to identify what your objective is before you start to network. This will make you more effective. Perhaps you want to further your career, create sales opportunities, make more friends or take a hobby to new level.

Networking requires patience; when you feel you're not getting anywhere, this is often when you strike gold with a contact who is a door-opener to a new opportunity.

Much networking can be done online via social media platforms and forums, such as LinkedIn, Facebook, Twitter and Instagram. Set your profile description as bait for those you might want to attract and research the hashtags that will reach out to them, or to find the influencers you seek. Send personalized messages explaining why you want to network with them. Be thick-skinned if not everyone responds to your requests to connect.

Never underestimate the power of face-to-face networking. Think about which national or local networks, clubs or societies you might join and what they have to offer. Attend events they hold; arrive early to talk to others attending before the main item begins, stay around afterwards to maximize opportunities to meet new contacts or talk to speakers and organizers. Be brave and bold about this; after all, what do you have to lose?

Don't forget to come with business cards, with your contact details and memorable message or strapline included—something that will stand out about what you do long after your initial meeting.

MAKE A DECISION

Making the right decision can be full of responsibility. It can be the difference between success and failure, or favoring a morally decent course of action over personal gain. Others may be affected or the decision, once taken, could be irreversible.

Fear of the outcome can make people timid about making a decision—this can drag out the decision-making process, sometimes resulting in a lost opportunity. By all means mull over the possibilities, but don't lose too much momentum.

Look objectively at a decision to be made by formulating a plan. List pros and cons in two separate columns for decisions that are straight choices between two options. Committing these to a list, rather than leaving them to swirl around in your head, can focus your thoughts and speed up the process.

Where there is a range of alternatives to consider, list these too and add some questions. For example:

- Who will it affect and how?

- What are the consequences now and in the future?

- What could go wrong?

Look further than the immediate solution that presents itself, as it won't necessarily be the best. Gather all the information to help you decide. Take professional advice where appropriate. Discuss any dilemmas with neutral parties and factor in their reactions and advice. Even just voicing the options to others can lead you to think differently about the decision.

DEFEND YOURSELF IN AN ARGUMENT

We all get yelled at from time to time. When it happens to you, seemingly out of left field, it can be hard not to snap back automatically.

Try hard to listen to what is being said to you, without interruption. Bristling with anger yourself and reacting badly could escalate the problem. Look for logic. Does your verbal attacker have a point? Is there something that you have done, even unwittingly, that might have caused upset? In which case, a quick and sincere apology normally works better than an attempt to justify your actions.

You may be facing a serial fight-picker desiring your reaction, even to the point of wanting your negative attention. If you react defensively to their opening complaint, the attacker is unlikely to back down—they'll continue with a long list of other related "sins" you have committed. Try responding in a way that doesn't allow them to carry on picking a fight.

Here are a couple of examples with different strategies to try.
"Why don't you make more of an effort about your appearance?" Tell a long, rambling story so they lose interest, that begins something like this, "That could be because of an incident that happened a long time back. One day…" "Why can I never find my phone? What have you done with it?" Respond with a neutral statement such as, "It can be very annoying when you can't find things." You may need to keep going with similar variations before your attacker runs out of steam.

GET BY IN A FOREIGN COUNTRY

Those of us who aren't natural linguists do better with a phrase book. Good travel guides often have sections covering how to greet people, how to say "please" and "thank you" and how to ask about transport, tourist information, accommodation and emergency facilities. Lists of local dishes and regional specialities are helpful, too—even if English language menus are available, not all translations are intelligible.

Alternatively, Google Translate's app will give you phrases and word meanings in over 100 languages, but be aware that there's no guidance on pronunciation.

Language classes or home-based language learning are worth considering if you intend to spend a lot of time in one country, or plan to make frequent visits.

Do ask local people for help when traveling. Most are happy to assist and a lot can be achieved with a few words and some judicial pointing.

It's a good idea to look up key etiquette points for the countries you are traveling to. This will safeguard you from causing offence unwittingly. Understand tipping policies and clothing etiquette—such as the requirement to remove your shoes before entering a mosque, to only wear shorts in Vietnam while on the beach, and so forth.

Going beyond the bounds of manners can land you in serious trouble with the authorities; for example, photographing airports, or military and government buildings.

There are additional etiquette rules when doing business internationally that can be deal-breakers if not observed, so make sure you're aware of these before you go.

HOW TO
DINE ALONE

It's worth doing your research before committing to a restaurant. Apart from looking for a menu that appeals to you, search for an atmosphere that you will be relaxed and comfortable in, an environment that is not noisy and frenetic and for staff that might look after a lone diner well. Decide on going out to eat early if you want to be quick and unobtrusive.

If you would rather not sit in isolation, choose a casual eatery with a communal table. In Amsterdam, for example, many restaurants have a shared table policy, so if you come in on your own you can dine in the company of others.

Ask for a table facing out into the room so you can see what is going on. Resist being led to a poorly positioned table just because you're alone.

Don't allow yourself to be put off by other diners; they are usually too engrossed in their own conversations and dining experience to notice others.

Dietary experts expound that you should focus on your food while you eat, without distractions. However, you may enjoy observing your fellow diners, or you might prefer to bring a form of entertainment along with you—a book, magazine or newspaper, or a sketchbook if you prefer, to fill the time before your food appears. Puzzles and crosswords can be less intrusive than fiddling with your mobile phone, or have a notebook and pen handy for thoughts that occur as you eat.

HOW TO
ENJOY YOUR OWN COMPANY

It's important to know how to enjoy daily life without needing to spend time with others. There may be periods in your life when you live alone, you're not in a close relationship or friends and family aren't on tap. Being self-reliant is a good platform to rest upon—or it can be the launch pad to explore new possibilities.

Besides the ability to entertain yourself, it's good to have some thinking time to reconnect with your own thoughts and values or to allow space for creativity to flourish. However, be wary of aimless TV watching, gaming and fixing on social media as a substitute for companionship. It's OK to waste time alone, particularly when you're tired, but putting a little planning into it can help you enjoy your downtime more.

Start to think of time alone as a positive thing. Working out what you enjoy doing and indulging in those activities when you have time to yourself is the first step. Some of these may be home-based, like listening to your favorite music, reading, cooking or painting; others involve getting out—for instance, trying a different sport or rediscovering a former passion.

Or be adventurous! Take yourself to see a town or city new to you, have a day out by the sea or in the country, or go to the cinema or a gallery. The sense of pleasure and achievement from getting out on solo activities can be immense.

FINAL WORD

If you've got this far and absorbed your new knowledge, congratulations! You should be better equipped than most to deal with what life throws at you.

Enjoy your new-found skills and be confident that you're in good shape in the kitchen, trim in the clothing department, a cleaning and household wonder, competent with two tires and four, safe in the great outdoors, a first-aid stalwart, superbly organized, socially adept and in possession of a set of people skills that are second to none.

INDEX

THE ART OF GOOD
CONVERSATION:

PEOPLE SKILLS:

IMAGE CREDITS